TWAYNE'S MASTERWORK STUDIES
Robert Lecker, General Editor

THE SCARLET LETTER: A READING
Nina Baym

THE BIBLE: A LITERARY STUDY
John H. Gottcent

MOBY-DICK: ISHMAEL'S MIGHTY BOOK
Kerry McSweeney

THE CANTERBURY TALES: A LITERARY PILGRIMAGE
David Williams

GREAT EXPECTATIONS: A NOVEL OF FRIENDSHIP
Bert G. Hornback

Heart
of
Darkness

Search for the Unconscious

Gary Adelman

Twayne Publishers • Boston
A Division of G. K. Hall & Co.

HEART OF DARKNESS:
SEARCH FOR THE UNCONSCIOUS

Gary Adelman

Twayne's Masterwork Studies
No. 5

Copyright © 1987 by G. K. Hall & Co.
All Rights Reserved
Published by Twayne Publishers
A Division of G. K. Hall & Co.
70 Lincoln Street, Boston, Massachusetts 02111

Designed and produced by Marne B. Sultz
Copyediting supervised by Lewis DeSimone
Typeset in Sabon with Garamond Italic display by Compset, Inc.

Printed on permanent/durable acid-free paper
and bound in the United States of America

Library of Congress Cataloging in Publication Data

Adelman, Gary.
  Heart of darkness.

  (Twayne's masterwork studies ; no. 5)
  Bibliography: p.
  Includes index.
  1. Conrad, Joseph, 1857–1924. Heart of darkness.
2. Imperialism in literature.   3. Africa in literature.
4. Congo River in literature.   I. Title.   II. Series.
PR6005.04H4738   1987   823'.912   86-29488
ISBN 0-8057-7953-1
ISBN 0-8057-8006-8 (pbk.)

To Phyllis

Contents

Note on References and Acknowledgments

All references to *Heart of Darkness* are taken from the Norton Critical Edition of the novel (New York: Norton, 1971), first published in 1963.

I would like to thank Barbara Horne, Herbert Marder, Norma Marder, and Phyllis Rider Adelman for having helped me achieve greater precision in the final draft. I also wish to acknowledge the help of Zohreh Sullivan and Robert Shuman for their readings of the manuscript. I would like to thank Charles Stewart for having read and responded to the section on imperialism. I also wish to thank Louise Crane and Dale Kramer for valuable suggestions. The frontispiece and the map drawings are the work of Carlton Bruett, who designed them for this book. I also wish to thank the English Department office staff, and particularly Anne Moore, for the typing of early drafts of the manuscript, as well as the Research Board of the University of Illinois for its most generous support. Finally, I am indebted to my wife, Phyllis Rider Adelman, for her scrutiny of the manuscript and dedication to its completion.

Chronology:
Joseph Conrad's Life and Works

1857   3 December. Józef Teodor Konrad Korzeniowski born in Ber-
        dyczów, a city in Russian-occupied Poland, now in the Soviet
        Ukraine; Poland then under Russian, Prussian, and Austrian
        control since the partition of 1793. Father, Apollo, of landless
        nobility, family having lost its estates in 1830 rebellion
        against Russia. Apollo is a poet and translator of Shakespeare
        and Victor Hugo, and author of plays attacking wealthy
        landowning classes.

1861   Apollo moves to Warsaw to help form National Central
        Committee, controlling organization of Polish resistance to
        Russia. In October, Józef and his mother, Ewa, arrive in War-
        saw; Apollo arrested as revolutionist and imprisoned.

1862   9 May. On evidence of Ewa's letters to Apollo, both are con-
        victed and deported, with four-year-old Józef, to Vologda in
        northern Russia.

1863   National Central Committee directs last great Polish insur-
        rection. Aleksander Poradowski among many Poles who em-
        igrate; his wife later helps Conrad get command of Congo
        River steamboat.

1865   April. Ewa, thirty-two, dies of tuberculosis, leaving Apollo in
        despair. Józef, subject to migraines and nervous fits, reads
        Shakespeare, Walter Scott, James Fenimore Cooper, sea
        stories by Captain Marryat, tales of exploration by Mungo
        Park, Hugo's *The Toilers of the Sea*, Dickens, Thackeray.

1868   Apollo and Józef permitted to return to Poland; settle in
        Cracow.

1869   Apollo dies of tuberculosis. Józef leads funeral procession; all
        of Cracow attends as tribute to national hero. Tadeusz Bob-
        rowski, Józef's maternal uncle, assumes responsiblity for boy.
        Seeing Korzeniowskis as victims of fanaticism, Tadeusz, a
        lawyer and advocate of orderly development toward democ-
        racy, tries to obliterate Korzeniowski influence upon Józef.

1872   Emotionally unsettled, bored with Cracow school, Józef proposes going to sea. In effort to discourage the notion, uncle sends him on tour of Switzerland with tutor.

1874   October. Uncle consents to let Józef go to Marseilles, and gives him allowance of two thousand francs a year. Through distant relatives, puts Józef in contact with shipowner named Delestang. In December, Józef makes first voyage as passenger on *Mont Blanc* to Martinique.

1875   Sails as apprentice on *Mont Blanc* to Cap Haitien and Le Havre.

1876   July. Begins eight-month stint as steward, sailing to Caribbean and West Indies and earning first salary of thirty-five francs per month. Days on land in Cartagena, Colombia, and in Puerto Cabello and La Guaira, Venezuela, provide visual material for *Nostromo*.

1877   March. Under influence of ultraconservative Delestang, perhaps sails on *Tremolino*, gunrunning from Marseilles to Spain for Carlist cause. Quarrels with Delestang and loses his job.

1878   February. Deeply in debt from disastrous Spanish enterprise and having gambled away a borrowed eight hundred francs, Józef shoots himself in chest just before creditor arrives for tea. Uncle hastens to Marseilles, but tells everyone that Józef was wounded in a duel—the same account Conrad later gives his wife and friends. In April, as deck hand on British freighter *Mavis*, begins career of sixteen years with British merchant navy.

1880   28 May. Passes exams as second mate. In August, sails to Sydney as third mate on *Loch Etive*.

1881–1883   September 1881 to April 1883. As second mate on *Palestine*, sails to Bangkok and Singapore (the basis of "Youth").

1884   February. Second mate on *Riversdale*, sailing to Madras. Quarrels with captain and returns from Bombay to London on the *Narcissus* (the basis of *The Nigger of the "Narcissus"*). In December, passes exams as first mate.

1886   August. Becomes naturalized British citizen. In November, obtains Master Mariner's certificate.

1887   February. Sails to Java as first mate under the command of John McWhir, later immortalized in "Typhoon." From August until following January, serves as chief mate on the *Vidar*, trading among the islands between Singapore and

Borneo—the world re-created in his first two novels, *Almayer's Folly* and *An Outcast of the Islands*. These Malayan voyages, along with A. R. Wallace's *Malay Archipelago*, also contribute to making of *Lord Jim* and *Victory*.

1888   January. Gets first and only real command, of *Otago*, a small ship of ten, because of his timely presence in Singapore when its captain dies. His assertion of first command is the basis for "The Secret Sharer" and "The Shadow Line." As captain, he is ironically referred to as the Russian Count: wears black jacket and white waistcoat, fancy trousers, gray bowler, gloves, and carries cane with gold knob.

1889   March. Resigns command of *Otago* and returns to Europe to visit aging uncle who is ill. Waiting in London for entry to Poland, begins *Almayer's Folly*, but interrupts it to apply for command of steamboat from Belgian company for commerce in the Congo. Seeks support for position from Brussels relative, Aleksander Poradowski. After Poradowski dies, Józef is helped by widow, Marguerite, who is forty-two and a novelist. Begins intimate correspondence with her; always calls her "Aunt."

1890   June to December. On the Congo River, suffers immobilizing attacks of malaria and rheumatism, which recur intermittently thereafter. Also experiences psychological shock, later re-created in *Heart of Darkness*.

1891   Convalesces in London and Geneva. In November, sails as first mate of clipper *Torrens* from London to Adelaide, Australia, a journey repeated the following year to conclude his career in the British merchant navy.

1893   July. Visits uncle in Ukraine at Oratów. Resumes *Almayer's Folly* while waiting for new ship.

1894   Uncle Tadeusz dies. Józef sends novel, dedicated to his uncle, to London publisher Fisher Unwin. Edward Garnett, junior reader of the firm, becomes close friend and most important critic.

1895   April. Publishes *Almayer's Folly* to praise of eminent writers. Changes name to Joseph Conrad.

1896   Completes *An Outcast of the Islands*. In spring marries twenty-three-year-old Jessie George, a secretary from a large, poor family. Garnett objects, but Conrad calls his new bride "a very good comrade and no bother at all."

1897   *The Nigger of the "Narcissus"* serialized, but Conrad is close to poverty because of poor sales. In August, begins lifelong friendship and important correspondence with Cunninghame Graham, an idealistic revolutionary much like Conrad's father.

1898   Son Borys born. In May, begins ten-year friendship with Ford Madox Hueffer—later Ford Madox Ford—with whom he collaborates on several potboilers. Achieves greatest creative period during friendship with Ford. Moves to Pent Farm in southeast England to be near Ford, and starts *Lord Jim;* interrupts project in December to write *Heart of Darkness* in one month. Publishes *Tales of Unrest* ("The Idiots," 1896; "Karain," 1897; "The Lagoon," 1897; "An Outpost of Progress," 1897; "The Return," 1898).

1899   February to April. Publishes *Heart of Darkness* in *Blackwood's Magazine.*

1900   October. Publishes *Lord Jim.*

1902   Publishes *Youth, a Narrative, and Two Other Stories* ("Youth," 1898; *Heart of Darkness,* 1899; *The End of the Tether,* 1902).

1903   Begins *Nostromo,* interrupting dictation to Ford of *The Mirror of the Sea,* which he describes as a "book of rubbish to sell to a paper" (quoted in Najder 1983, 297). In April, publishes *Typhoon and Other Stories* ("Amy Foster," 1901; "Typhoon," 1902; "Tomorrow," 1902; "Falk," 1903) dedicated to Graham.

1904   Publishes *Nostromo.*

1906   Son John born. Publishes *The Mirror of the Sea, Memories and Impressions.*

1907   Publishes *The Secret Agent.*

1908   Publishes first volume of *A Personal Record.*

1909   Friendship with Ford ends rancorously. Wife, Jessie, ill.

1911   Publishes *Under Western Eyes.*

1912   Publishes *A Personal Record,* volume 2, and *'Twixt Land and Sea, Tales* ("The Secret Sharer," 1910; "A Smile of Fortune," 1911; "Freya of the Seven Isles," 1912).

1913   Publishes *Chance.*

1914   28 July. Conrad family arrives for vacation in Cracow the day Austria-Hungary and Serbia declare war. In Cracow Conrad composes political document urging England to recognize

Polish right to national unity. 10 October, departs Poland on train full of wounded Austrian soldiers. 2 November, arrives in London, having promised Polish patriot Marian Biliński to petition London papers to publicize Polish nationalist interests; however, he finds the press apathetic and the English government officially announces Poland's future to be Russia's internal affair. Conrad, in bad health, becomes bitterly pessimistic. The following January refuses invitation to join Relief Committee for War Victims in Poland.

1915   Publishes *Victory*.

1917   Publishes *The Shadow-Line*.

1920   Publishes *The Rescue*.

1923   Publishes *The Rover*. 1 May to 2 June, in New York and Boston at Doubleday's expense for lectures and publicity appearances. Received as popular celebrity, but in poor health.

1924   January. Grandson Philip born. In May, declines offer of knighthood from Ramsay MacDonald's Labour government, probably out of loyalty to Polish aristocratic title. 3 August, dies of heart attack. 7 August, buried with Roman Catholic services at Canterbury.

I

Historical Context

Heart of Darkness has one of the most profoundly pessimistic visions in Western literature. The thrust of all the works upon which Conrad's reputation stands is an elemental nihilism that mocks human endeavor. Its source is probably to be found in Conrad's personal history: his mother dead when he was seven, his childhood spent in a dreary wasteland of northern Russia, his father dead when he was eleven, and his ties to his homeland broken by voluntary exile when he was seventeen. At the age of twenty he attempted suicide by shooting himself in the chest. His experiences in colonial Africa probably deepened a cynical predisposition to "see things as they are." Between June and December 1890, Conrad worked for a Belgian colonial firm that had concession rights to the exploitation of ivory and rubber along a thousand miles of the Congo River. At the time he was in the Congo, the Belgian king was busy erecting his crudely effective machinery of exploitation: the awarding of concessions to ambitious firms, the decreeing of laws that impressed the Congolese into forced labor, and the creation of a military police force that ruthlessly punished those who refused to work or who sought to emigrate. Though these proceedings were not in their mature stage until the middle of the 1890s, Conrad witnessed firsthand much that was shocking; as a representative of the company, he must have felt complicity. More than three million Africans in the Congo died of European abuse during Leopold II's reign.

In his correspondence during the 1890s, and especially in his letters to Cunninghame Graham, one senses a personal conflict beneath the frequent outbursts of philosophical pessimism. In his dialogue with Graham, who reminded him of his revolutionist father, we hear him shouting down the voice of politically active idealism.

The fate of a humanity condemned ultimately to perish from cold is not worth troubling about. If you take it to heart it becomes an unendurable tragedy. If you believe in improvement you must weep, for the attained perfection must end in cold, darkness and silence. In a dispassionate view the ardour for reform, improvement for virtue, for knowledge, and even for beauty is only a vain sticking up for appearances as though one were anxious about the cut of one's clothes in a community of blind men. Life knows us not and we do not know life—we don't know even our own thoughts (14 January 1898, in Watts 1969, 65).

Conrad's knowledge of late nineteenth-century developments in astrophysics and evolutionary biology provided him with evidence and imagery appropriate to his nihilistic moods. Was the earth not formed from the coagulation of gases? And would it not end as a frozen, desiccated planet? And did human beings not originate from a long succession of accidental mutations leading to the ape? Ergo, all endeavor was useless. Life was a bubble organism that lasted a while, suffered, and burst. Of course, Conrad included in his general survey a mockingly cynical assessment of human affairs.

Conrad was attracted to the mood of romantic decadence in the English poets of the 1890s (W. B. Yeats, Ernest Dowson, Arthur Symons, D. G. Rossetti). His biographer, Frederick Karl, says he learned his literary English from these poets, whose exoticism and tone of ennui and exhaustion have been shrewdly described as "a yawn to stifle their cry of despair" (G. K. Chesterton, quoted in Watt 1979, 161). In *Heart of Darkness,* Conrad tried to stifle his own despair with the creation of Marlow. Marlow exemplifies Conrad's stand in the face of pessimism. Marlow's code is a seaman's code and, more generally, the code of the British ruling classes. He embodies the ideal of duty practiced automatically, like a reflex, in fidelity to the values of his society. Marlow stands by these values. To him they are a matter of faith; and we see from the frame story that Marlow the narrator is no less a trusted member of the elite than the young Marlow in his own narrative had been when naively setting off for Africa. Yet his story may make one wonder how this can be so, and how, for that matter, anyone could suppose Conrad to be endorsing his narrator's views. For in Africa, Marlow sees the truth about imperialism. His account of his experiences shows him confronting a political reality that undermines his faith in himself and the civilization he represents. However, what he ultimately chooses to understand is another matter.

Marlow's story projects a myth, the central feature of which is that the Victorian has had fostered within him a psychopathic craving for destruction, and that imperialism is an irremediable manifestation of this unconscious desire. Marlow confronts in the ivory trader Kurtz the fundamental motive of imperialism. In his acknowledgment that Kurtz is his alter ego, Marlow risks moral annihilation. Yet we see from the frame story that he has learned to shut his eyes and accept the status quo. It is also clear that Conrad himself clings to what his character represents, even to the extent of discriminating—through Marlow—between better and worse forms of imperialism. After his own Congo experience, Conrad had no illusions about the existence of a civilizing mission behind the Western penetration of Africa. But his account of the ugly truth of imperialism in *Heart of Darkness* is contained by the myth, with its implication that there is no remedy. No better option than reaffirming fidelity to the values of the British Empire is available in the novel's purview; Marlow, therefore, feels justified in believing that British imperialism is good. The alternative is nihilism. In *Heart of Darkness* there are but two choices: Kurtz's malignant egoism, or imperialism's organized savagery.

Conrad was one of many innovators of the 1890s who were interested in the rediscovery of the unconscious. It was a decade in which "[p]sychological process ... replaced external reality as the most pressing topic for investigation" (Hughes [1958] 1977, 66). Dostoyevski was the harbinger of this new literary period, and Conrad's characters—Marlow in *Heart of Darkness,* Jim in *Lord Jim,* and the captain in "The Secret Sharer"—greatly resemble Dostoyevski's in their subtle, psychological complexity. Marlow, in fact, is probably Conrad's most fascinating pyschological subject. He is presented to the reader in the act of vividly recollecting the way he saw things, and the reader participates in his experience, seeing as he does, yet seeing more of the whole story than Marlow is capable of seeing. What enables us to see through him and fathom his unconscious psychology is the novel's symbolic structure, its architectonics. Conrad probably derived his narrative method in *Heart of Darkness* from Henry James, who preceded him in perfecting the technique of telling a story through a central character's limited point of view. But the poetic mode of his presentation is derived from Dostoyevski. Thus the progress of the narrative is toward expanded moral awareness, with readers having the advantage of anticipating this progress because they are conscious of the novel's symbolic design.

The drama of Marlow's unconscious psychology, like that of Raskolnikov's in *Crime and Punishment,* is placed in a moral landscape that reveals the hero to himself. From it we learn why Marlow goes to colonial Africa and why Raskolnikov commits murder, and in it we see the unacknowledged inner self of Marlow, the upright Victorian, and of Raskolnikov, the atheist. Marlow does not become stupidly callous in Africa, like the chief accountant of the Coastal Station who resembles him in caricature, nor does he quite have a mental breakdown like his predecessor, Captain Fresleven. Rather, he confronts Kurtz as Raskolnikov confronts Svidrigailov. Kurtz is the depraved embodiment not only of the colonial process, but also of the civilized individual's destructive instinct. Similarly, Dostoyevski implies through Svidrigailov something equally prophetic—that this ruthless rapist and murderer is what people will become if faith in God dies out. In the world of Dostoyevski's novels there is an implicit, fanatical devotion to the idea of God, an obsessive insistence on its necessity. But in *Heart of Darkness* there is no such hope, no higher truth. Kurtz's Intended is no Sonia Marmeladova. Rather, she represents blind faith in the status quo. She is the reward that goes to imperialism's successful warriors. Because in the world of the novel there is no acceptable alternative to Marlow's commitment, *Heart of Darkness* is a prophetic vision of doom.

II

The Importance of the Work

Heart of Darkness is the most vividly realized account in literature of the experiences of a European in colonial Africa, and as such is a document of historical importance as well as a literary classic. It is also an exciting adventure story; but unlike *Gulliver's Travels*, or *Robinson Crusoe*, its true focus is not the exotic land being discovered by the reader, but rather the behavior and psychology of the English traveler, Conrad's narrator Marlow, as he copes with the moral dilemma he experiences in Africa. The impression that there is an underlying psychology to the enacted events of the story is conveyed symbolically by a variety of devices, including the use of a double. Conrad has mastered in the novel, which many regard as the first truly modern work of fiction in English, a highly suggestive narrative form that enables the reader to discover by inference what the author, as omniscient narrator, in the traditional novel communicates directly. Remarkably, Marlow's experiences in the Congo, which are presented in exhaustive and concretely visualized detail, stand forth in the imagination as a myth: a story of the human condition, tragically prophetic, and of our times, having political and metaphysical implications roughly analogous to central ideas found in Nietzsche and Freud.

The political dimension of the novel is rendered concretely by the narrative, which is Marlow's account of how he obtained command of a Congo River steamboat, and of what he saw, did, and felt on a journey to the furthest point of navigable trade along that river. It is the story of a decent young Englishman who enlists, for the adventure, in an enterprise heralded as opening a backward part of the world to civilization, but who finds himself participating in the brutal exploitation of Africans. Instinctively he tries to conceal the truth from himself that some part of him is excited by the license to commit savagery. He revolts from seeing that as an employee of the colonial company, he cannot maintain a posture of moral superiority. But his posturing intensifies his feelings of isolation and anxious foreboding. Vaguely understanding that to Europeans in Africa, morality and survival are incompatible, he is unconsciously attracted to a colonizer who has accepted reality. This is a man who plunders the region for ivory at the head of an army of Africans who adore him as their god. But this Mr. Kurtz, who has accepted the truth about the real motives of imperialism's "civilizing" mission, is no model for the hero, even as an example of how to survive. He is insane and dying. The hero himself nearly dies, his moral constitution undermined by the spiritual shock of having been unable to imagine an acceptable alternative to his predicament. He returns to Europe depressed and cynical, his youth destroyed by the truths he has learned about human nature.

Heart of Darkness consists of the subjective impressions of the narrator Marlow as he vividly recollects his experiences in Africa. But his record of sensations and thoughts does not represent the groping of a mind toward the truth about imperialism. Rather, it shows a mind struggling for the means to accommodate itself to that ugly truth. Toward this end Marlow begins to lie and to distort reality, and we observe him in these maneuvers. They are vain efforts on his part to maintain moral superiority.

Conrad creates a symbolic framework for this drama of moral breakdown, in which Marlow's account represents something like a casebook study of a young man succumbing to the unconscious motive that has transformed his fellow Europeans into colonizers. The function of Kurtz, the various metaphorical uses of darkness, the recurring motifs—all the symbolic paraphernalia—reinforce this interpretation by suggesting the nightmarish truths being disclosed to the hero, truths that have implications. The story is one in which the political theme illustrates a vision of tragic prophecy: Western civilization is driven by an unconscious need to dominate others and to destroy itself. The novel reveals this unconscious psychology in a decent European by dramatizing his struggle to suppress knowledge of his real reasons for having gone to colonial Africa. As the internal pressure mounts—because the hero is pandering to unacknowledged desires—he externalizes his anxiety and begins hating the persecuted Africans as corrupting influences. In doing so he exonerates himself from the consequences of his own behavior should he lose control. *Heart of Darkness* is monumental in being the first great work of literature in which a characteristic feature of the colonial experience— severe ideological trauma—is subtly and indelibly recorded.

The frame story, which introduces the narrative, also functions as an afterword in which Marlow is depicted as a trusted member of the English elite. It is implied that he has passed through a spiritual crisis, and has made his commitments: he stands for Victorian values and the British Empire. In effect, the frame story attaches a moral to Marlow's narrative: that however imperfect civilization may be, the alternative to preserving its values is worse. The alternative leads to a revolt against common decency on grounds that its claims are hypocritical and emasculating. Bertrand Russell's great admiration for Conrad was based on what he read in *Heart of Darkness* to be its uncomfortably honest vision of the truth of the human condition, and to what he interpreted to be Conrad's implicit distrust of all political "isms" and religions aspiring to improve it. Russell writes that Conrad "thought of civilized and morally tolerable human life as a dangerous walk on a thin crust of barely cooled lava which at any moment might break and let the unwary sink into fiery depths" (1967, 321). By contrast, there is a school of Marxist thought that finds *Heart of Darkness* important for a different reason: it stands as an example of a modern author's falsification of political reality.

III

Critical Reception

Questions and Issues

*H*eart *of Darkness* is intriguing, like *Hamlet* or like a Kafka novel, in that readers taken by the power of the story never feel quite satisfied with their attempts to intellectualize the experience. Perhaps the most basic of the puzzling questions is whether Conrad is ambivalent in his attitude toward imperialism. Does he know his own mind, or is the story an exploration for him, no less than for Marlow? Can one say that Conrad is ironic in his attitude toward the primary narrator, the one who prepares the stage for Marlow's narration by raising a glowing tribute to England's colonial empire while the brooding gloom of a sunset settles over its capital city? How, one asks, can he be anything but ironic? Marlow's story is about nothing if not the savagery of colonialism. But, then, how can one explain Marlow's continuing on as an agent of the company, clear-sightedly abetting "robbery with violence," persevering against all the claims of decency to the furthest point of navigable trade? Is not a fascinating psychology subtly revealed in the way Marlow relates to the other agents and to the wilderness? The reader sees nothing save what is registered through Marlow's sensibilities; but what appears masterful as technique in the limited point of view—Conrad in control, building his effects out of the subjective impressions of his central character—appears altogether puzzling in the light of the suspicion that something so entirely personal is being recorded that Conrad himself is not altogether aware of what he is revealing. Does or does not Marlow feel, as he moves further into the interior, "visceral revulsion" (Parry 1983, 30) for the Africans? Do we not see his grasp of reality gradually become distorted out of fear for himself, and mortification over his own duplicity, and out of the need to exonerate himself from blame? If, as some

8

critics believe, Marlow is to be seen undergoing severe mental trauma, and that what happens to him is a typical feature of the colonial experience, is not Conrad, through Marlow, recording the unconscious imprint of his own Congo experience? If so, how can Conrad at the same time be said to have ironic distance from Marlow?

The climax of the story is Marlow's meeting with Kurtz. What power of fascination and symbolic content does Kurtz represent in the journey to the "heart of darkness"? Does Marlow discover in him the embodiment of his own unconscious motives for having come to Africa? Is Kurtz the symbol of Marlow's own "heart of darkness"—an embodiment of the destructive instinct of the European psyche that has made a voyeur, if not altogether a colonizer, of Marlow, and that has made a great slave plantation of Africa? If so, what then is the meaning of Kurtz's famous deathbed cry, "the horror"? If a judgment on his own savage actions, it is by implication an exhortation for inculcated social restraints. If this is the meaning, how can Marlow call such a cry "an affirmation," since in the logic of the novel it is the pressure of civilized restraints that has created both the irrepressible, subconscious, destructive urge responsible for the carving up of Africa *and* the cloak of moralistic hypocrisy? Is Kurtz, who has experienced the satiety of primitive emotions, reacting instead to "the horror" of having to die? And is he thus expressinga lust for life that civilized people are incapable of experiencing inthe gray torpor of what they call existence? Can we say whatMarlow learns from Kurtz—in what sense he is exposed, enlightened, shocked—if we do not have a sure sense of what Conrad means by Kurtz's "summing-up whisper"?

Marlow's lie to Kurtz's Intended draws the curtain on the story, and is far too important to be described as officious, a little white lie told to a grieving woman who wanted and insisted on hearing it. Why does Marlow suppress the truth about imperialism? How can one explain his perverse insistence on a claim of loyalty to Kurtz's memory? But is it really loyalty to Kurtz that prompts his lie? What explanation can artistically justify the melodramatic rendering of this final scene? And finally, seeing that Marlow is presented in the frame story as enlightened by his experience, what is hinted, or can we suppose implied, about the way he has learned to live with truth? Has Marlow become a skeptic who, notwithstanding his nihilistic vision, recognizes the necessity of social restraints? Or is Conrad implying something other than enlightenment by Marlow's pose in the frame story—cross-legged like a Buddha—namely, despairing resignation?

These crucial questions have led to the conceptualizing of all kinds of imaginative frameworks, theories, and approaches in efforts to account for the experience of the novel. In the more than eighty years since its publication, *Heart of Darkness* has been read, to quote Benita Parry, "as an attack on imperialism, a parable about the construction of ethical values, a mythic descent into the primal underworld, a night journey into the unconscious self and a spiritual voyage towards transcendent knowledge" (1983, 20). Some of the more important and stimulating commentaries are presented in the following pages.

Early History

Heart of Darkness first appeared in serialized form in the conservative *Blackwood's Magazine* for the months of February, March, and April of the year 1899. In a letter of 31 December 1898, Conrad sketches the idea of his novel: "The title I am thinking of is 'The Heart of Darkness.' . . .The criminality of inefficiency and pure selfishness when tackling the civilizing work in Africa is a justifiable idea. The subject is of our time distinctly—though not topically treated. It is a story as much as my *Outpost of Progress* was but, so to speak 'takes in' more—is a little wider—is less concentrated upon individuals" (quoted in Sherry 1973, 129). In a letter written 8 February 1899, to R. B. Cunninghame Graham, Conrad warns his socialist admirer that issues other than colonialism are of importance in the novel. Delighted with his friend's response to the first installment, he writes: "You bless me indeed. Mind you don't curse me by and bye for the very same thing. There are two more installments in which the idea is so wrapped up in secondary notions that You—even You!—may miss it. And also you must remember that I don't start with an abstract notion. I start with definite images and as their rendering is true some little effect is produced. So far the note struck chimes in with your conviction—mais après? There is an après" (Watts 1969, 116).

Heart of Darkness was published in book form by William Blackwood in 1902. The volume entitled *Youth* contained three works: a short story by that name; *Heart of Darkness*; and a second short novel, *The End of the Tether*. The popular press reviews concentrated on "Youth" and glossed over *Heart of Darkness*. Reviewers suggested that it was intended for an elite audience, and that it would mystify the general public. Edward Garnett's review in *Academy and Literature* (6 December 1902) was undoubtedly the most perceptive reading of the text. He called *Heart of Darkness* "the high-water mark" of Conrad's talent, and said that "the art of 'Heart of Darkness' implies . . . the acutest analysis of the deterioration of the white man's *morale,* when he is let loose from European restraint, and planted down in the tropics as an 'emissary of light' armed to the teeth, to make trade profits out of the 'subject races'" (quoted in Sherry 1973, 132). Garnett comes close to seeing the novel as an exploration of the Western psyche.

The poet John Masefield, who reviewed the book for the *Speaker* (31 January 1903), did not respond to the issues raised by Garnett. He criticized Conrad for having failed to fully realize Kurtz, whom he took to be the central character. He found the style, though brilliant, altogether too rhetorical and contrived. His judgment of *Heart of Darkness* is summed up in the words "too much cobweb" (quoted in Sherry 1973, 142). On the whole, between 1900 and 1910 reviewers were more attracted to the companion pieces "Youth" and *The End of the Tether.*

Marlow and Kurtz

Joseph Warren Beach was one of the earliest of Conrad critics to appreciate Conrad's genius at suggesting the unconscious psychology of his characters. Yet despite the comparison Beach makes between Conrad and Dostoyevski, he fails to see Marlow as other than a technical device with which Conrad subtly and impressionistically condemns imperialism, or Kurtz as other than a symbol of its evils. Beach writes:

> Kurtz was to Marlow, penetrating this country, a name, constantly recurring in people's talk, for cleverness and enterprise. But there were slight intimations, growing stronger as Marlow drew near to the heart of darkness, of traits and practices so abhorrent to all our notions of decency, honor, and humanity, that the enterprising trader gradually takes on the proportions of a ghastly and almost supernatural monster, symbol for Marlow of the general spirit of this European undertaking. The blackness and mystery of his character tone in with the savage mystery of the Congo, and they develop *pari passu* with the atmosphere of shadowy horror. This development is conducted cumulatively by insensible degrees, by carefully calculated releases of new items, new intimations; and all this process is *controlled* through the consciousness of Marlow. Thus we have a triumph of atmospheric effect produced with the technique of the limited point of view, a story in a class with "The Fall of the House of Usher" and "The Turn of the Screw." (1932, 343–44)

Douglas Hewitt was one of the first critics to interpret *Heart of Darkness* in terms of Marlow's struggle against acknowledging kinship with Kurtz. He sees Marlow as the central focus of the novel—Marlow in revolt against truths that remain hidden from him until his meeting with Kurtz. Until this point he retains standards by which he criticizes the traders, and asserts that he is different from them. With Kurtz, however, Marlow cannot deny kinship: "He accepts the bond established between them, just as he has accepted the bond between himself and the savage clamour from the river bank on the journey upstream," and this dark bond of sympathy with Kurtz opens his eyes to the temptations he has experienced, and to the dimensions of the evil he has seen. ([1952] 1969, 24–25).

Albert J. Guerard contends that what Marlow is narrating is a therapeutic voyage of self-discovery into his own unconscious. He argues that the story's authenticity lies in its dreamlike contours—the sensation, or atmosphere, of nightmare enveloping the tale—and that Marlow's "night journey" is a symbolic bid for partial relief from a "crippling solitude and normal human condition" ([1958] 1979, 48). The potentially integrating self-revelation of the story occurs, Guerard says, when Marlow discovers an entity within himself symbolized by Kurtz, who is his double, and who represents "the Freudian id or the Jungian shadow or more vaguely the outlaw" ([1958] 1979, 39).

The Meaning of "The Horror"

Ian Watt suggests that Kurtz's death cry is the answer to an unspoken question that had been growing in Marlow to an increasing desperateness: "How can man, and especially civilised man, be and do what he has seen?" (1979, 240). Watt says further, summarizing what is probably the most generally accepted interpretation of this climactic moment for Marlow, "The horror is seen as a verdict on the essential depravity of man and his civilisation," and "the main object of Kurtz's condemnation is surely himself, and what he has done" (236).

Lionel Trilling, by contrast, regards Kurtz as "a hero of the spirit." Kurtz dares to experience existential freedom, preferring its truth "to the bland lies of the civilization that has overlaid it" (1965, 21). His deathbed cry is no moral judgment on the inherent depravity of human nature, and hence an affirmation of the necessity of socially inculcated restraints. Rather, it is the despair of a passionate man resigning himself to death, and "to Marlow the fact that Kurtz could utter this cry at the point of death, while Marlow himself, when death threatens him, can know it only as a weary grayness, marks the difference between the ordinary man and a hero of the spirit" (1965, 20).

K. K. Ruthven shares with Trilling a Nietzschean perspective on the novel:

> Everything turns on the interpretation of this cry . . . is it a deathbed renunciation of an evil life, as the narrator and some critics would like to believe, or is it (as Marlow suspects) simply exultant, a confirmation of the unspeakable and an unrepenting re-

jection of the European values Marlow cherishes? It is possible to regard Kurtz as the hero of this story because he not only has the courage to reject the obsolete values of a dying civilization, but risks destruction by facing the unknown and tackling it on its own terms; and if Kurtz is the hero, *Heart of Darkness* is implicitly an attack on the values of western society and an annunciation of the Savage God. The clue to all this is the way in which Conrad describes Europe and Africa, for the choice Kurtz is required to make is not between a good Europe and a bad Africa but between two different kinds of badness: Kurtz must choose between the mausoleum of Europe and the wilderness of Africa. (1968, 41)

Robert F. Haugh interprets Kurtz to be a Nietzschean hero (Nietzschean in the sense that Lev Shestov writes of the German philosopher—as a saint in the making) and interprets Marlow's fascination to be with

a hero who had shown him the limits of the mortal spirit. . . . His remarkable energies, his stature, his amazing appeal to fellow humans in his moments of darkest savagery, the very magnificence of his plunge into the pit of the universe, all these showed Marlow a moral universe, dark though it was. Emerson's line: "Yawns the pit of the Dragon, Lit by rays from the Blest" indicates the nature of this final, blinding illumination: "that could not see the light of the candle, but was wide enough to penetrate all the hearts of the universe." This is why, to Marlow, Kurtz is a true hero; a vision downward, dark, may be as true as a vision upward into the light. . . . In his remarkable actions he defines the mortal condition, and in his last moment of vision he sees all the scheme of the universe; and we share it in a moment of tragic exaltation. (1957, 54–55)

The Meaning of "The Lie"

In a novel in which the central character recounts his experiences of European imperialism, it is jolting to have as a final scene the hero suppressing the truth of what he has seen. No aspect of the text has attracted as much critical attention as has Marlow's lie to Kurtz's Intended. The context of the scene itself implies an obvious explanation—that of the white lie—but such an explanation can hardly be called a satisfying closure to a novel that is concerned ultimately with Marlow's progressive enlightenment. Even if we embellish the duplicity, arguing that he lies to the Intended because he has learned the value of love from his experiences while nearly lost in the hell of his own egoism, and thus that his lie is an act of charity to a bereaved woman in the true Christian sense of the word, the explanation still does not make for a satisfying sense of closure. By having Marlow lie to the Intended, Conrad undermines the novel's essential meaning, which is found in the hero's reluctant but ultimate acknowledgment of the reality of imperialism.

Jeremy Hawthorn suggests that it is not the horrifying details of Kurtz's career that oblige Marlow to lie to the Intended. Rather, he is forced to lie by a feeling of identification with Kurtz, which has him duplicating Kurtz's relationship with the Intended to the extent that he is sexually attracted to her and feels obliged "to reproduce her illusions for her" (1979, 33). What accounts for this feeling of identification, Hawthorn says, is the climate of imperialism. Marlow is the product of an imperialist society, and as an Englishman with "the right instincts," he cannot admit to the barbarianism of Westerners in Africa. He is compelled to participate "in reproducing the half-ignorance upon which imperialism thrives" (1979, 35). Thus, his lie—which is "the final 'knitting in' to the complicities of imperialism of Marlow himself" (33). Similarly, Benita Parry sees the lie as the denouement to themes "valorising the doctrine of cultural allegiance as a moral imperative which is independent of the community's collective moral conduct. It is to this end that the adumbrations of racist views, the denigration of a foreign structure of experience and the commendation of submission to civilisation's discontents are directed, strategies that clear the way for sanctioning Marlow's lie in defence of Europe" (1983, 36).

Eloise Knapp Hay, by contrast, perceives Marlow as the naive, unwitting witness of evil who, once conscious of his complicity, behaves superbly. By his lie to the Intended, he is acknowledging his identification with Kurtz and silently confessing his guilt. Hay interprets the lie as a symbolic act analogous to Oedipus's putting out of his eyes. The lie represents Marlow inflicting punishment upon himself for complicity in crimes against humanity ([1963] 1981, 158).

Thomas Moser regards the lie as the satisfying closure to a story essentially concerned with Conrad's struggle to confront the source of his sexual inhibitions. Kurtz is Marlow's fantasy of sexual abandon. By his act of loyalty to Kurtz—the lie—Marlow shows that he has partly conquered his sexual inhibitions and has learned to be less afraid of self-abandon. The lie, "Marlow's reaffirmation of fellowship with Kurtz" (1957, 81), suggests a Marlow less afraid of losing himself.

H. M. Daleski agrees with Moser that Marlow has been struggling to be less afraid of abandon. But he interprets the lie as Marlow's attempt to conceal his admiration of Kurtz's savage woman, who is symbolic of a crucial fact of life, which neither Marlow, nor Conrad, is able to accept: that examples of primitive vitality exist that are not destructive. Daleski's thesis is that Conrad is invariably struggling in his fiction to learn the lesson that true self-possession is based on a "capacity for abandon." Conrad and Marlow fail to learn the lesson in *Heart of Darkness*: hence, the lie (1977, 75–76).

Aesthetic Judgments

Although Conrad is regarded by most critics as a literary genius who, in his cadenced prose, occasionally reminds one of Milton, he has other, more grudging admirers who criticize him for being limited, pretentious, and obscure. Virginia Woolf found occasion to write of Conrad in 1924, the year he died. She takes issue with the critics who find him difficult, and points out that what makes him difficult to read—his beauty of style—is what makes him magnificent. "One opens his pages and feels as Helen must have felt when she looked in her glass and realised that, do what she would, she could never in any circumstances pass for a plain woman" (1925, 310). Nevertheless, Woolf reserves this tribute for Conrad's writings about the sea because, according to her, Conrad is passionately interested only in characters who are scaled by large values—"fidelity, compassion, honour, service" (317); consequently he requires an elemental and heroic world in order to be inspired:

> He [Marlow] had sat upon deck too long; splendid in soliloquy, he was less apt in the give and take of conversation; and those "moments of vision" flashing and fading, do not serve as well as steady lamplight to illumine the ripple of life and its long, gradual years. . . . It is the earlier books—*Youth, Lord Jim, Typhoon, The Nigger of the "Narcissus"*—that we shall read in their entirety. For when the question is asked, what of Conrad will survive and where in the ranks of novelists we are to place him, these books, with their air of telling us something very old and perfectly true . . . will come to mind. . . . Complete and still, very chaste and very beautiful . . . as, on these hot summer nights, in their slow and stately way first one star comes out and then another. (317–18)

In essence, Woolf judges Conrad a great minor writer incapable of creating a psychological and social reality, which is the novelist's primary responsibility. She praises him to the sky, but for doing one thing—and only one thing—well.

E. M. Forster's admiration for Conrad is seldom recalled because his cutting remarks are more memorable. He writes that Conrad is: "misty in the middle as well as at the edges, that the secret casket of his genius contains a vapour rather than a jewel; and that we need not try to write him down philosophically, because there is, in this particular direction, nothing to write. No creed, in fact. Only opinions, and the right to throw them overboard when facts make them look absurd. Opinions held under the semblance of eternity, girt with the sea, crowned with the stars, and therefore easily mistaken for a creed" ([1936] 1955, 131).

Forster's irritation at Conrad's pomposity is mitigated by boundless admiration for Conrad's genius as a stylist. Also, Forster puts his finger on the very reason for his exasperation with Conrad: namely, that Conrad's great fiction has a nearer and a further vision that are mutually contradictory. What Conrad affirms, he undermines at another level in the narrative. Forster, in his more generous moments, confesses that Conrad is a genuine visionary.

F. R. Leavis "canonized" Conrad for the very reasons Woolf criticized him. He places Conrad in a tradition of great English-language novelists all of whom (including Jane Austen, George Eliot, and Henry James) are masters in the art of social and psychological realism. But he finds *Heart of Darkness* difficult to grasp concretely, and marred throughout by "an adjectival and worse than supererogatory insistence on 'unspeakable rites,' 'unspeakable secrets,' 'monstrous passions,' 'inconceivable mystery,' and so on" ([1948] 1954, 218).

IV

Situating the Text

Conrad's Development as a Writer

Conrad was twenty when in 1878 he sailed as deckhand on the British freighter *Mavis,* which carried coal to Constantinople, and began a career of sixteen years in the British merchant navy. In 1880 and 1884, he passed his exams as second and first mate, and voyaged to Sydney; to Sumatra (the basis of his adventures aboard the *Palestine* described in "Youth"); to Madras, returning to London from Bombay aboard the *Narcissus* (the basis of *The Nigger of the "Narcissus"*); and to Singapore. Two particularly notable events occurred in 1886: in August he became a naturalized British citizen, and three months later he obtained his Master Mariner's certificate. He was, however, with one exception, to find it impossible to secure a command. Between 1883, the first time British tonnage under steam exceeded that being moved by sail, and 1894, the year Conrad's career as a seaman ended, even though the total tonnage of ships increased by 25 percent, the actual number of merchant ships diminished by half; and it has been estimated that while Conrad was in the British merchant navy, an average of 260 masters lost employment every year.

Conrad sailed to Java in February 1887 as first mate under the command of the imperturbable John McWhir, later immortalized in "Typhoon." From August 1887 to January 1888, he sailed as chief mate of the *Vidar,* which traded with the islands between Singapore and Borneo. He was to re-create the world he was discovering on these voyages in his first two novels, *Almayer's Folly* and *An Outcast of the Islands,* and later in *Lord Jim.* The only real command he ever obtained was that of the *Otago,* a small ship with a total complement of ten, which came his way because he happened to be in Singapore when its captain died. He took command in January 1888 (the assertion of his first command being the basis of "The Secret Sharer" and "The Shadow Line") and resigned it in March 1889, when he returned to Europe in order to visit his aging uncle, who was ill.

In London, while waiting for clearance to visit Poland and finding it impossible to get work, he began writing *Almayer's Folly*. The novel, however, was interrupted by the most improbable of adventures. The British press was giving the African continent and its explorers extensive coverage, and Conrad, envisaging the fulfillment of a childhood fantasy—"When I grow up I shall go *there*" (pointing smack at the center of the continent) (*A Personal Record* 1924, 13)—applied to Albert Thys, the director of the Belgian Company for Commerce in the Upper Congo, for command of one of the Congo River steamboats. He also wrote to Aleksander Poradowski, a distant, well-connected cousin, for his help in securing the position with the company. In February 1890, he visited the Poradowskis in Brussels on his way to Poland. Aleksander died two days after his arrival; but Conrad made the acquaintance of Aleksander's wife, Marguerite, who became his intimate correspondent for the next five years. She was an attractive, cultured woman, and the author of two novels published in the prestigious *Revue des deux mondes*. Her efforts on his behalf paid off, and in April 1890 he returned to Brussels, the company's headquarters, to secure his appointment.

One can gather from *Heart of Darkness*, which Conrad wrote eight years later, that the Congo experience transformed him. He was later to tell Garnett that before the Congo journey, he "was a perfect animal" (introduction to *Letters* 1928, 8). Evidently he was shocked by what he saw and did in Africa, and if the novel is an indication, the shock was psychological, spiritual, even metaphysical. Although Conrad was in the Congo scarcely six months (from June to December 1890), he was forever after regularly afflicted by severe attacks of malaria and rheumatism, and "by bouts of disabling physical illness or psychological prostration" (Watt 1979, 126).

Edward Garnett, who was later to become his editor and one of his most insightful critics, and Gerard Jean-Aubry, his first biographer, thought the African experience made Conrad into a writer. Indeed, "we have not only *Almayer* in incubation but a career of thirty years" on his return to Europe (Karl 1979, 310). In 1891, he spent time in a London hospital and in a sanatorium near Geneva.[1] In November, after waiting vainly for a command, Conrad accepted an appointment as first mate of the famous passenger ship, the clipper *Torrens,* which sailed from London to Adelaide. Two long ocean voyages to Australia, the first in 1891 and the second in 1892, were to be the last in his career in the British merchant navy. He left the *Torrens* in July 1893, paid a last visit to his uncle in the Ukraine, and, while looking around for another ship, resumed work on *Almayer's Folly.* The work on the novel continued while he was in Rouen in the post of first mate of the *Adowa,* which was chartered to carry emigrants to Canada, but which never crossed the ocean. In his biography, Frederick Karl notes that knowledge of Conrad's reading during these sea years is incomplete (1979, 267). He does mention with some confidence that Conrad was reading from the French symbolist poets, specifically Baudelaire and Mallarmé, and from Flaubert, Maupassant (*Pierre et Jean*) and Turgenev. Conrad probably also read the work of Pierre Loti during this period, as well as Yeats and the first writings of Herman Melville, "about whose early work" Karl writes, "he was enthusiastic" (349).

Early in 1894, Conrad's Uncle Tadeusz died. By then, *Almayer's Folly* had been creeping along for four years, although he had spent the greater part of the preceding five months working on it, and would spend another three months completing it. In July 1894, Conrad sent his novel to the London publisher Fisher Unwin. Unwin's junior reader, Edward Garnett, liked it, and Conrad received an offer for the book. Garnett, who was to become a close friend, was just beginning a career of discovering new talent. Conrad was one of a number of his discoveries, who included James Galsworthy, W. H. Hudson, and D. H. Lawrence.

Józef Teodor Konrad Korzeniowski adopted the name Joseph Conrad, by which he is generally known, with the publication of *Almayer's Folly* in April 1895. Karl says, "As much as Yeats and Dowson, Conrad learned his literary English at the end of the century, and was only able to make it leaner and more pungent as he developed a more mature style. For him, this would come at the end of the 1890s" (1979, 350). Stylistically, *Almayer's Folly*, with its cloying atmosphere of languor and exhaustion, is a prose counterpart of fin-de-siècle poetry. Thematically, the novel resembles Flaubert's *Madame Bovary*. Stretching the point somewhat, one can see the novel as a version of *Madame Bovary* set in Borneo. Conrad's declared masters, Flaubert and Maupassant, were formative influences in his learning of the craft. Conscientious art is what won his enthusiasm, especially in the works of Maupassant's master, Flaubert. Ian Watt writes of this indebtedness:

> Conrad departed from the Victorian tradition of the intrusive author in favour of Flaubert's attitude of narrative impersonality and emotional *impassibilité* towards his creation; and he also adopted Flaubert's ideal of artistic completeness in the rendering of a single unified theme. The most specific aspect of his likeness to Flaubert can be seen in the way that, both in *Almayer's Folly* and his later fiction, Conrad proceeds through an exhaustive and primarily visual presentation of each aspect of the central subject. (1979, 53)

In short, Flaubert's will to style compelled Conrad's admiration: style for its own sake—the sound of a phrase, the cadence of a paragraph, the effect of concrete details wholly visualized that enable the reader to see and feel without being told. Flaubert's attitude toward his creation in *Madame Bovary* is entirely aesthetic. One senses a cold, satiric amusement, as if the god of Emma Bovary's world were taking a ribald pleasure in the reality he was creating. There is no pity or sentiment in the Flaubertian point of view. Conrad admired the cold mirth, the sense of pitiless inevitability, the absence of indignation, and indifference to political allegory, just as he admired the lucid, distanced irony of Maupassant—because it was expressive of his own attitude toward the world.

In 1896, Conrad completed a second novel, *An Outcast of the Islands*. From the very onset of his literary career, he received the praise of writers of eminence, an extraordinary feat for a Polish refugee who was ignorant of the English language until the age of twenty. In the next fifteen years he was to achieve for himself the first place among modern English writers of fiction, alongside James Joyce and D. H. Lawrence.

In the spring of 1896, Conrad married twenty-three-year-old Jessie George. She was a secretary from a large, poor family. She had little formal education and no interest in literature. Garnett tried to dissuade Conrad from what appeared to be an obvious misalliance, but Conrad nonchalantly assured him that his new bride was "a very good comrade and no bother at all" (*Letters* 1928, 48). He appears to have married Jessie in order to arrange his life in a manner that would enable him to conserve himself for the excruciating labor, as he would put it, of turning "nervous energy into phrases." For him, the honeymoon months alone with Jessie in Brittany constituted perfect conditions for consistent work. *The Nigger of the "Narcissus"* (the first of a handful of such minor masterpieces as *The End of the Tether,* "Typhoon," "The Secret Sharer," and "The Shadow Line") was begun during these early months of his marriage and represents a giant step forward in his development of a tighter, leaner, prose style, and of a unified symbolic structure.

Many of Conrad's biographers (Morf, Meyer, Karl) remark on the considerable guilt he must have felt as he moved inexorably toward a career as an English writer, "even to the extent of marriage to an English girl" (Karl 1979, 367), while his ties to Poland receded. The psychological function of art, according to Meyer, is the achievement "of a corrective revision of a painful reality" (1967, 8). Conrad's early life is used by these critics to intuit his psychic history—the unresolved conflicts and suppressed nightmares that energized his art and became the obsessive themes of his fiction. In part, the need to explore his inner life led Conrad to Henry James and ultimately to the creation of Marlow. He was an admirer and reader of James certainly as early as 1896 (Karl 1979, 383). Between 1896 and 1898, James perfected the technique of registering the experience of the novel as a whole through the subjectivity of a protagonist. Of the four works in which Conrad utilizes Marlow as a central intelligence, *Chance* (1913) is a mediocre imitation of James; and the other three, "Youth," *Heart of Darkness,* and *Lord Jim,* were written between the summers of 1898 and 1900, the two years following James's perfection of his experiment in point of view. Conrad admired the inimitable way James manipulated point of view and presented shifting perspectives on a single incident. Through the subjective impressions of an intermediary struggling with hard truths, Conrad was able to explore his own feelings without exposing them. Marlow was Conrad's way of evading direct confrontation with his neuroses. And Marlow enabled Conrad to develop rapidly his mature style: a narrative consisting of shifting angles of ironic perspective about certain key events. These events seem to be accidents of fate, but are actually dramatic representations of the inner psychology of the central character unconsciously working itself out.

The writer Conrad most resembles in his mature fiction is Dostoyevski. Though he never tired of expressing his dislike for the Russian (both on patriotic and artistic grounds), in no other writer do we come so near to Conrad's architectonics—the turning of plot into a poetic representation of the central character's psychic life. Joseph Warren Beach was one of the first of Conrad's commentators to point out this resemblance. Like Dostoyevski, he writes, "Conrad was much concerned with twists and puzzles of psychology—growing out of the character's *Weltanschauung*"; both shared "a profound feeling of the mysteriousness, the almost transcendental character of human motives" (1932, 340).

Two friendships appear to have had profound impact on Conrad's development as a writer. Cunninghame Graham initiated a lifelong friendship in August 1897 by writing Conrad about "An Outpost of Progress" (published in book form in *Tales of Unrest,* 1898). The work itself is mediocre, a first stab at the material of *Heart of Darkness,* and the only other story Conrad wrote based on his Congo experiences. The most interesting of Conrad's letters belong to his correspondence with Graham—letters in which we sense Conrad in touch with deeply inhibited feelings (refracted into bursts of philosophic and poetic pessimism) during his tremendous creative surge at the turn of the century. In many ways, Graham was like Conrad's revolutionist father: an aristocrat, politically radical and idealistic, driven by a need to challenge authority and, in the process, to stir up trouble. Karl suggests that Conrad's "own well-hidden anarchistic tendencies, his own sense of rage and chaos carefully buried under the skin, were allowed freer play because of Graham's presence" (1979, 395).

But of all Conrad's friends during his growth as an artist in the 1890s—Garnett, Galsworthy, H. G. Wells, and Graham—no relationship was so important as that which developed in May 1898 between him and Ford Madox Hueffer. Hueffer, later known as Ford Madox Ford, was nine years younger than Conrad, an aristocrat at home in artistic circles, and already the author in his early twenties of a novel, a book of poems, and a biography. During a ten-year friendship, the two collaborated in writing a number of potboilers. More important, Ford was a compatriot in the profession—someone to whom Conrad could talk about the special needs of the craft. Even more significant is the fact that Ford seems somehow to have helped Conrad work with all the power of his focused imaginative resources; quite independently of their collaborative efforts, Conrad wrote all his masterpieces during the decade of their friendship—*Heart of Darkness, Lord Jim,* and *Nostromo,* as well as *The Secret Agent.* Meyer believes that Ford must have enabled Conrad to dare a profound self-analysis, the sort we understand Marlow to be confessing to in confronting his double, Kurtz. Some such "spiritual union," Meyer believes, existed between Conrad and Ford, "which len[t] to Conrad, at least, a certain boldness in his willingness to search his inner self" (1967, 167). It is very curious, as Meyer remarks, that Conrad "rarely displayed this quality before he knew Hueffer," and that "he was destined to show it with decreasing frequency following the dissolution of their relationship" (167). In October 1898, Conrad moved to Pent Farm in the southeast corner of England to be near Ford; here he began to write *Lord Jim,* which he interrupted in December to write *Heart of Darkness,* completing the forty-thousand-word novel in one month.

Nineteenth-Century Imperialism and the Making of Heart of Darkness

During his months in Africa, Conrad was the employee of a Belgian colonial trading company, Société Anonyme Belge, that was exploiting the Upper Congo for raw materials, particularly ivory and rubber. The Congo itself, some eighty times the size of Belgium, was the personal property of the Belgian king, who was in the process of developing the crudely effective machinery of exploitation when Conrad arrived in 1890. What precisely Conrad saw is to some extent a matter of conjecture. The observations in his diary at the time do not reveal an acknowledgment of any blatant European abuse of Africans. Nevertheless, there is no dispute as to what King Leopold II was doing in the Congo, and therefore as to what Conrad must have seen. In part, *Heart of Darkness* is a reexamination of that past, a probing for the truth about imperialism and of what the author had seen and participated in while working for the Belgian company. I say "in part" because the novel is hardly an account of the hero Marlow's progressive enlightenment. Rather, it is foremost a subtle psychological portrait of a man's retreat from truth in his struggle against moral collapse. Marlow is eventually to have his moment of truth, but it is doubtful that he, or for that matter Conrad, fully understood the implications of what had happened to him. In an effort to absolve himself of responsibility for what he sees and does working for the company, Marlow begins to hate and blame the Africans for what the Europeans are doing to them. Without acknowledging it to himself, Conrad's naive, well-meaning hero has discovered that he cannot maintain his dignity and survive in a racist colonial environment; therefore, though posturing to himself and to others, he makes the necessary adjustments, imperceptibly becoming a racist himself. But if the novel's demeaning depiction of Africans and its insinuation that Europeans are corrupted in Africa is seen as central to Marlow's moral breakdown, and if the moral breakdown itself is seen as ideologically significant—a feature of the archetypal colonial experience—then it is wrong to attack Conrad for racism in *Heart of Darkness*.[2] There are, however, reasons to believe that Conrad is ambivalent in his attitude toward imperialism: despite his firsthand experience of Belgian colonialism—for that matter, despite his having cruelly suffered from Russian colonialism in Poland—his anger and clarity of focus are for some reason neutralized in *Heart of Darkness*. His hero Marlow suppresses the truth of what he has seen in Africa; and years later, in the present time of the frame story, he fraternizes with English company men aboard a sailing yawl.

Heart of Darkness reflects contradictory feelings about imperialism. Not only was the nineteenth century an age of nationalist (which meant imperialist) rivalry among European powers in the "scramble for Africa," but Conrad may also have been particularly susceptible to the climate of English imperialist fervor and national pride at the time he wrote *Heart of Darkness*. In December 1898, England was on the verge of war with Germany, a nation Conrad hated, as he hated Russia, for having partitioned his homeland.

Nothing helps further a sense of intimacy with the text than placing the novel concretely in the political reality of Conrad's time: the context of nineteenth-century European imperialism. The following section describes events leading to the Berlin Conference of 1885, which "legitimized" European domination of Africa while making Leopold a gift of the Congo. This history, especially Leopold's exploitation of the region, serves as a prologue to an account of Conrad's actual journey in 1890 from Boma, at the mouth of the Congo, to and from Stanley Falls, twelve hundred miles upriver. The chapter concludes with a description of the climate of political bias in England at the time Conrad wrote *Heart of Darkness*.

Leopold Gets the Congo.   The true center of *Heart of Darkness* is the subtly revealed psychology of an ethical human being struggling to maintain a moral perspective—a sense of moral cleanliness, at any rate—in a situation revoltingly immoral. Colonialism in central Africa is the political reality of the novel, but this world is experienced through the sensibilities of an individual undergoing trauma from his struggle against moral collapse. The imperative, the tantalizing question of why the hero Marlow remains in the employ of the colonial trading company, and appears incapable of taking a moral stand, is answered indirectly by the example of three colonizers who suffer experiences similar to Marlow's, the last of whom Marlow recognizes as the incarnation of the unconscious motive that brought him to Africa in the first place. The black mood of the story grows out of the hero's inability to accept the truth about colonial exploitation. He acquires a tragic vision from the climactic, shattering experience of being unmasked as just another European colonizer in Africa.

The vision is tragic because it implies a metaphysical conception similar to Freud's conclusion in *Civilization and Its Discontents*—namely, that the inhibitions that are the bedrock of civilized, communal life have created a powerful death wish within the civilized ego, an instinctual need to dominate or to be destroyed. Because this need is irrepressible, the "scramble for Africa" must be understood as part of the psychic fee humans pay and will continue to pay (in ever more terrible tragedies) for the privileges of civilization. The central focus of this nightmare is on the illuminating distortions we are given of the wilderness and of Africans. Marlow's bizarre depiction of the Africans of the interior makes sense only as a feature of the hero's mind at the point of breakdown, and probably this evidence of trauma is an unconscious imprint of Conrad's own colonial experience.

In its broadest sense, imperialism means the domination of one group over another. We can see in retrospect that from its beginnings with the "Age of Discovery" in the fifteenth and sixteenth centuries, imperialism meant the Europeanization of the globe. Soldiers, merchants, adventurers, missionaries, and pilgrims of religious sects were the vanguard of colonizers of the new worlds. The "Age of Mercantilism" during the seventeenth and eighteenth centuries ushered in an era of colonial wars among the European nations, jockeyings for power, and prescriptive ownership of such lucrative dependencies as India and Egypt. In the nineteenth and twentieth centuries, the "Age of Imperialism," the motives and methods of the European powers for staking claims reached a new level of sophistication (Baumgart 1982, 10–11).

Until the nineteenth century, Africa was an unexplored continent because it was of little interest to the European powers. More than 90 percent of its trade was in slaves from the Atlantic coast. European interest in the continent was a spin-off of the legitimate trade that was introduced as the abolition of slavery took effect. The search for raw materials (mainly vegetable oils) brought in merchants, adventurers, and eventually missionaries. As the continent was explored, the European powers sought to develop markets for their manufactured goods. England, the undisputed empire-builder, had demonstrated in India how valuable a dependent, populous market could be to the economy of the mother country: it imported raw materials from the subcontinent at throwaway prices and sold manufactured goods to it at cutthroat rates. In addition to the financial profit of occupying colonies, there was the political advantage that enhanced the prestige and influence of the nations on the European continent. The exploration of Africa soon gave rise to rivalry among European powers who wanted to absorb the Dark Continent. A corollary to the principle of the balance of power in Europe was the notion of a "colonial balance in Africa." This meant that none of the nations was allowed to extend its power either in Europe or abroad to the extent that it threatened other nations by becoming dominant in a region of conflicting interests. During the last quarter of the nineteenth century the "scramble for Africa" began in dead earnest. Conflicting commercial interests between Britain and France in the Mediterranean and on the east and west coasts of Africa sparked off a rivalry in which other countries joined, motivated by a feeling that they could no longer afford to confine their interests to the continent of Europe.

The explorer Henry Morton Stanley exacerbated the tensions of the rivals. In 1871, and again in 1876–77, he penetrated the rain forests from Zanzibar to the lower Congo, and in the process traced the full course of the Congo River. Stanley's discovery of the importance of the river, which he encouraged England to exploit as "the grand highway of commerce in West Central Africa," precipitated a crisis that threatened to upset the European balance of power (Legum 1961, 16). The region the river opened—extending from the Atlantic Ocean over the Congo basin to the foothills of the Ruwenzori Mountains—was nearly the size of Europe. It had been decimated by slavery.[3] In the years of flourishing slave trade fifty thousand men, women, and children were imported to the New World annually, and the number carried off by Arab traders was much higher. In all, as many as 13 million lives were destroyed—about twice the population of modern Zaïre. In the 1870s, Stanley encountered vast depopulated areas. The tribes and their clans survived in fearful isolation and practiced cannibalism "on a scale unknown in other parts of the continent" (Legum 1961, 27). Stanley's idea was that England should make a colony of this pitiable country, and build a railway line from Matadi, 80 miles from the coast, where the river became unnavigable, to Kinshasa, 230 miles upriver, where the waterway was clear for navigation 1,000 miles into the interior. Stanley pictured trading posts extending the whole length of the river: of a Congo Basin open to commercial trade, with the ocean readily accessible to the transport of the country's rich resources of rubber and ivory. But he was frustrated by Britain's rebuff of his grand scheme. Liberal policy under William Gladstone preferred that Britain not own the Congo, but make sure that control of it pass into the "right" hands, that freedom of commerce be guaranteed, and that the internal slave trade be vigorously combatted. The valuable mineral deposits of the southwest region, the Katanga, had not yet been discovered. Britain preferred that the Congo be controlled by Portugal. Her chief rivals, France and Germany, however, had other ideas; Leopold II, king of Belgium, had yet other visions of his own. It was to Brussels that Stanley was lured after England rebuffed him, where Leopold soon contrived to exploit every ounce of the explorer's talent.

Leopold's public life was directed by the late nineteenth-century nationalistic ideal of creating, through the possession of colonies, a richer, more powerful Belgium. As crown prince, he tried to buy an Argentine province. When he became king in 1865, he tried to obtain leases in Mozambique and the Philippines. In 1875, responding shrewdly to the escalating interest in Africa, he called for an international conference, held in Brussels, for the purpose of forming the Association Internationale Africaine and of becoming the association's president. Leopold addressed the conference as a humanitarian: "The slave trade, which still exists over a large part of the African continent [the reference is to Arab slavers, and to the institution of domestic slavery], is a plague spot that every friend of civilization would desire to see disappear. The horror of that traffic, the thousands of victims massacred each year . . . the still greater number of perfectly innocent beings who, brutally reduced to captivity, are condemned *en masse* to forced labour . . . makes our epoch blush." (quoted in Legum 1961, 14–15). Lest anybody should think him ambitious for Belgium, he assured the conference. "No, gentlemen: if Belgium is small, she is happy and satisfied with her lot" (Legum 1961, 18). The king then offered to pay out of his own pocket the cost of opening up the Congo to civilization: that is, to stamp out slavery, to make the country accessible to trade, and to put it at the disposal of the European powers. It was ostensibly for this purpose that Leopold, in his capacity as president of the Association Internationale Africaine, sent Stanley to negotiate treaties with African rulers in the Congo that would open the way for peaceful commerce and occupation, and for the building of the railway line to which Leopold pledged a part of his private fortune. Between 1879 and 1884, Stanley made exploratory expeditions into the interior of the Congo, set up trading posts, and made more than a hundred treaties with tribal chiefs. The chiefs "surrendered any right to levy tolls, or dispose of the natural resources in their territories; they ceded the right to cultivate unoccupied lands, to exploit the forests, to fell trees, and to gather all natural products." They were also obliged to "furnish labour, and to join forces against 'all intruders of no matter what colour' " (Legum 1961, 28). The chiefs were obliged because they feared white men and their superior military power. They were also persuaded that positive benefits might accrue from collaboration with these agents of European civilization; and, ironically, they were promised protection from the internal slave trade. In the name of the Association Internationale Africaine, the region was being opened as a "free trade" area; but in reality it was a commercial sphere of interest to be exploited by the association. Leopold had a flag designed to denote the sovereignty of the allegedly philanthropic association in the region, but no one mistook it as other than the emblem of a purely private commercial enterprise.

In 1881, tensions began to heat up when the Anglo-Portuguese treaty was signed. The treaty was attacked in England, Germany, and Holland on grounds that the Portuguese would not eliminate slavery, and would hinder "the cause of Protestantism" (Legum 1961, 19). France ignored the treaty and moved aggressively into the area. Because the powers were headed on a collision course, they agreed to the German chancellor's suggestion for a conference at which to discuss the claims and disputes over the Congo Basin and other matters arising from the European rivalry for African real estate. The Berlin Conference, held from 15 November 1884 to 26 February 1885, was attended by all the principal rivals in the "scramble for Africa." The powers sought "to recognize or define the jurisdiction in Africa of the International African Association, or of France, or of Portugal, or of some other power, or to reconcile the rivalries and conflicting claims of each and all" (Perry Belmont, quoted in Legum 1961, 22). It is a curious historical parenthesis to note the part that the United States played in helping Leopold to a supreme coup—absolute monarchical control over a piece of Africa eighty times the size of his own country. He succeeded in persuading General Henry Sanford, the American ambassador to Brussels, to resign in order to become associated with the enterprising African organization. Shortly after Sanford became Leopold's agent, the United States recognized the flag of the Association Internationale Africaine as that of the Congo, a friendly government; this act of recognition, by a nation that itself had abstract claims to the region owing to Stanley's American citizenship, helped to persuade the great powers to facilitate the framework within which King Leopold developed the Congo Free State. The king was successful, however, for other reasons, not the least of which was Belgium's small size, which made her a safe buffer between the other European rivals for the Congo. In Leopold's hands, the territory was neutralized, while its "free trade" status was maintained, in principle, by the granting of equal trading concessions to the European states. In the end, the Berlin Conference not only settled the problem of the Congo, but also acknowledged existing spheres of European influence, and established ground rules for the carving up of the rest of Africa.

The Congo Free State was established in 1885. Between 1885 and his death in 1908, Leopold II was its supreme executive and legislative authority. The Belgian parliament ratified the decision of the Berlin Conference to make the Congo his personal property. His maneuvers had borne fruit. The Association Internationale Africaine had indeed come of age. Leopold was entrusted with a domain of nine hundred thousand square miles. Because the Congo was not claimed as a possession of Belgium (for the new state of the Congo was the king's personal estate), Leopold had only his private fortune with which to create a colonial administration. By 1889, having done nothing to establish the basic structure of a civil administration, and with a railway line (his one personal effort at capital improvement) scarcely off the drawing board, Leopold had depleted his personal fortune, and had but nominal control over the country. He had established a military presence, explored the terrain of his colony, and defined its borders. Following the example of his French neighbors, one of his first acts (in July 1885) had been to make himself owner of all the unoccupied land, which he proceeded to parcel out as concessions to ambitious firms for exploitation and governance in his name. These concessionaires, many of which existed only on paper, and which, in reality, were controlled by Leopold, "were given monopoly rights to the collection of rubber, ivory, palm oil, and other natural products" (Legum 1961, 29). It became a crime for the indigenous population to trap a bird or hunt in the forests outside the villages. Very quickly the Congo was divided up into districts controlled by administrators working either for Leopold or for private concessionaires who were compelled to pay twice: an outright fee for the concession, and a tax for collecting what was in the land. By 1889, having erected an enormous machinery for exploitation by force, Leopold's men turned to boosting the exploitable exports in the colony. "The overriding consideration was more rubber and more ivory" (Legum 1961, 29).

The Congo Free State was rapidly being turned into a great slave plantation. Because labor was scarce, Leopold sanctioned the impressment of labor by decreeing that administrative officers could take whatever steps they needed in order to work their territories profitably. He assisted by levying a labor tax, which indentured the Congolese to spend one quarter of their workaday lives toiling at minimum payment for his agents. Immediate and dire punishment was inflicted upon those who resisted, for the Force Publique, which was established in 1892, enforced the law by severing the hands, and sometimes a hand and a foot, of "rebels."

Rubber was ingeniously obtained. In 1899, a state official described to a British consular officer his method of rubber collection:

> [The] procedure was to arrive in canoes at a village, the inhabitants of which invariably bolted on their arrival; the soldiers were then landed, and commenced looting, taking all the chickens, grain, etc., out of the houses; after this they attacked the natives until able to seize their women; these women were kept as hostages until the Chief of the district brought in the required number of kilogrammes of rubber.
>
> The rubber having been brought, the women were sold back to their owners for a couple of goats a-piece, and so he continued from village to village until the requisite amount of rubber had been collected. (Anstey 1966, 6)

In 1890, when Conrad was in the Congo, work had started on the railway line that was designed to open the interior to European exploitation. From the onset, the project was beset with difficulties. The terrain was rocky and labor hard to find. The Bakongo had bad experiences working as porters on the caravan trail between Matadi and Kinshasa. The Europeans had used force to keep them at work, and had paid them only a franc and a half a day. By 1890, they had deserted the region. Leopold employed workers from other African colonies, establishing a pay scale of one shilling a day. He permitted the purchase of slaves, and in fact he worked in collusion with the notorious Arab slave trade that he had promised to stamp out. It was also common practice for his agents to conscript into chained work gangs so-called criminals. These railway workers lived in miserable conditions. When low wages, near starvation diet, illness, and fatigue finally exhausted them, they retreated, by one account, to a hill just above the town, where they died. Official Belgian figures report that of the forty-five hundred who worked on the railway between January 1890 and May 1892, nine hundred—some 20 percent—died. Reliable sources estimate that between 1892 and 1907, more than 3 million Congolese died from European abuse.

As far as Leopold was concerned, the colony was profitable. Between 1893 and 1900, its revenue rose from 5.5 million to 26 million francs. By 1901, its revenue reached 31 million francs. The money was used in Europe to finance museums, to beautify Brussels, and to provide edifying public works.[4]

At the turn of the century, Leopold's practices were beginning to be exposed. The protest was greatest in Britain, where the Congo Reform Association was under the leadership of E. D. Morel, the author of *Red Rubber*. A British exposé, based largely on the reports of Roger Casement, a British consul in the Congo, documented the horrors perpetrated in the region. Demands were made that the king be relieved of his exclusively personal rule over the Congo. Finally, on 28 August 1908, the Belgian parliament took over the Congo from their king. Reform was slowly implemented.

Conrad in the Congo.   Through the influence of a distant, well-connected relative in Brussels, Conrad managed to secure an appointment with the SAB (Société Anonyme Belge)—the Belgian company for commerce on the Upper Congo. Owing to the death of a captain, Freiesleben, of the S. S. *Florida,* one of three SAB steamers servicing company trading posts along the thousand miles of river between Kinshasa and Stanley Falls, Conrad was verbally promised a command. The contract he signed at the company's home office in Brussels committed him to serve for three years as an officer on river steamboats.

Apart from his general excitement at the prospect of participating in the exploration of the Congo, it is quite probable that Conrad believed in the idea of imperialism's civilizing mission when he embarked from Bordeaux on 10 May 1890. He shipped out aboard a French steamer, the *Ville de Maceio,* which made calls at various African ports, among which were Grand Bassam on the Ivory Coast and Grand Popo in Dahomey (later noted in *Heart of Darkness*); reached Boma, fifty miles upriver from the Congo estuary, 12 June; and proceeded thirty miles farther up to Matadi, the most distant navigable port on the lower stretch of the Congo. Matadi was an important colonial post. One hundred seventy Europeans lived there; four factories had been established in addition to the SAB station; and construction had begun on the railway line. Conrad was detained there two weeks, employed packing ivory into casks and searching for Africans to work as porters for the 230-mile trek to Kinshasa. During the delay in Matadi, he made two diary entries which, while they make no mention of ill-treatment of the Africans or a "grove of death," clearly imply that he was disturbed by what he saw. In the first entry of the *Congo Diary,* he records this uneasiness, as well as the favorable impression made upon him by Roger Casement, whose report, thirteen years later, as a British consular officer, was to expose the full dimension of labor abuse in the Congo. Casement knew the coastal languages well, and was apparently sympathetic to the plight of the Africans. Conrad's entry, dated 13 June 1890, reads: "Made the acquaintance of Mr. Roger Casement, which I should consider as a great pleasure under any circumstances and now it becomes a positive piece of luck. Thinks, speaks well, most intelligent and very sympathetic. Feel considerably in doubt about the future. Think just now that my life amongst the people (white) around here cannot be very comfortable. Intend avoid acquaintances as much as possible" (*Congo Diary,* 7).

In attempting to ascertain what Conrad actually experienced, Zdzistaw Najder, the most scrupulous of Conrad's biographers, reminds us that the real question (for Conrad no less than Casement, who was supervisor of the railway construction in 1890), is not so much what was happening there, but how it was understood. One knows, for instance, the working conditions and mortality rate of the African construction crews on the railway line; and one also has, as Hunt Hawkins informs us, the eyewitness report of George Washington Williams, an Afro-American journalist and historian who was in the Congo at the same time as Conrad, and who became the first outspoken critic of Leopold's regime (1982, 166). But again, the question is not what Conrad saw; rather, it is how he understood it: did he find Africans stupid savages unwilling to contribute to progress, or poor wretches worked to death (Najder 1983, 128)? It is evident from Williams that Conrad also saw cannibalism and human sacrifice as practiced by the Africans. Najder, who believes Conrad was disgusted and increasingly isolated by his experience of European colonial practices, thinks he did not make such observations in his diary because notes of that sort would have been superfluous for the purpose of refreshing his memory. All the notations in what Najder looks upon as a writer's diary are limited to details of topography, climate, and the like, and to very specific personal impressions. Yet it also seems possible that Conrad, as a representative of the company, shunned recording evidence of colonial abuse for reasons of prudence as well as (in light of *Heart of Darkness*) of guilt.

On 28 June Conrad set out with another SAB employee, Prosper Harou, and thirty-one porters, on the overland passage to the port of Kinshasa, where Conrad had expectations of becoming skipper of the S.S. *Florida*. The party made the 230-mile crossing in thirty-five days, with a seventeen-day rest midway at Manyanga. The terrain they crossed was gruelingly difficult: chains of hills, deep gorges, wooded ravines, broad plains of tall grass, many rivers. The party habitually broke camp at 6:00 A.M. and walked, during the morning hours, in weather that varied from "infernally hot" to "remarkably cold," an average of about twelve miles. To Conrad, the grueling terrain and the seediness of his and Harou's health made the distance seem considerably longer. Owing to European abuse, Africans living along the caravan trail had largely deserted, and only occasionally were there village marketplaces with eggs and chickens for sale. The long rest at Manyanga suggests that Conrad may have been dispirited as well as ill. His concluding entry, as the caravan arrived at the port of Kinshasa on the dawn of 2 August, reads: "Mosquitos. Frogs. Beastly. Glad to see the end of this stupid tramp. Feel rather seedy. Sun rose red. Very hot day" (*Congo Diary*, 15).

At Kinshasa, Conrad found that the steamboat *Florida* had been wrecked, and that the SAB manager of the station had become exasperated by his long delay. An immediate antagonism developed between the men: Conrad, thirty-two, recent commander of the oceangoing *Otago*, thoroughly the gentleman and aristocrat by temperament; and Camille Delcommune, thirty-one, soured by the misfortunes of a wrecked steamer and a recent damaging fire to company property. The day after his arrival in Kinshasa, Conrad departed for Stanley Falls aboard the SAB steamer *Roi des Belges*, which left in haste in its course of provisioning company stations and relieving agents, to aid a disabled troop carrier that belonged to the state. Conrad was obliged to leave promptly to seek guidance from a captain skilled in the navigation of the river, and the second part of his diary, begun with the upriver journey, consists of notes and sketches of the river.[5] The Congo River was extremely difficult to learn, measuring as wide as ten miles—"a huge, elongated lake, interspersed with islands and shoals" (Najder 1983, 134)—tapering to a twisting, meandering waterway of shallows and snags. On the whole, the region of the Upper Congo was sparsely populated—not more than six African villages over a span of five hundred miles—while here and there the *Roi des Belges* passed European and Arab trading posts. Conrad, on the bridge with Captain Koch, was occupied with taking notes during the twenty-eight-day, thousand-mile voyage to Stanley Falls, the last town on the upper part of the river that could be reached by steamer. He arrived 1 September at what had become a great center for ivory since the time that Stanley had established the trading post in 1883. A Dutch commercial house was in fierce competition with the SAB, and Arab slavers in the area were doing a flourishing business.

At Stanley Falls, where the steamer relieved Georges Antoine Klein, an SAB agent suffering from dysentery, both Conrad and Koch took ill with the disease. On the return trip, the steamer left on 7 or 8

September, with Conrad in command probably until Bangala, halfway to Kinshasa. En route, on 21 September, Klein, who is Conrad's obvious source for Kurtz, died. Aside from his being a commercial agent, his dying of dysentery, and his being buried along the river, no evidence indicates that a deeper resemblance existed between Klein and Kurtz. At Kinshasa, Conrad discovered that Camille Delcommune had no intention of making him a skipper of one of the SAB steamboats. Two days after his arrival, in a letter of 26 September to Marguerite Poradowska, he writes:

> No point in deceiving oneself! I definitely regret having come here. I regret bitterly. . . . I find everything repugnant here. Men and things, but especially men. And I am repugnant to them, too. . . . The director is a common ivory-dealer with sordid instincts who imagines himself a merchant while in fact he is only a kind of African shopkeeper. His name is Delcommune. He hates the English, and I am of course regarded as one. While he is here I can hope for neither promotion nor a raise in salary. Anyhow, he told me that promises made in Europe are not binding here unless they are in the contract. (quoted in Najder 1983, 137)

Najder believes that the root of the enmity between Conrad and the manager of the station at Kinshasa was Conrad's contempt for the company's colonial practices, and Delcommune's hatred for a company employee who was not "reliable." Though bitterly disillusioned, Conrad had no legal grounds for breaking his contract; and so he lingered in Kinshasa, vainly hoping for command of the ship of an exploring expedition that was under the leadership of Camille Delcommune's brother, Alexandre. These two brothers are sources for the especially caustic depictions in *Heart of Darkness* of the manager of the Central Station, and of the uncle of the manager and leader of the Eldorado Exploring Expedition.

Between 26 September and 19 October, Conrad suffered another attack of dysentery, which provided him with a legal way out of his contract. He left Kinshasa on 19 October, and, forced to retrace the grueling overland journey, fell desperately ill. Six weeks later, on 4

December, he arrived at Matadi, barely six months after he had come to the Congo. There is no record of when he actually sailed from Boma. Toward the end of January 1891, he appeared in Brussels, and on 1 February he was in London.

The letters he wrote at the time to his cousin and patron, Marguerite Poradowska, and to his uncle, Tadeusz Bobrowski, are full of complaints. His diary proper, from 13 June to 1 August, consists of jottings about his movement, the terrain, and the physical circumstances of the day's march; the entries he kept from 3 to 18 August consist of his notes on the navigation of the river. The entry for 4 July, for instance, is typical:

> Left camp at 6h A.M. after a very unpleasant night. Marching across a chain of hills and then in a maze of hills. At 8:15 opened out into an undulating plain. Took bearings of a break in the chain of mountains on the other side. Bearing NNE. Road passes through that. Sharp ascents up very steep hills not very high. The higher mountains recede sharply and show a low hilly country. At 9:30 market place.
>
> At 10h passed R. Lukanga and at 10:30 camped on the Mpwe R.
>
> Today's march. Direction NNE ½N. Dist[an]ce 13 miles.
>
> Saw another dead body lying by the path in an attitude of meditative repose.
>
> In the evening three women of whom one albino passed our camp. Horrid chalky white with pink blotches. Red eyes. Red hair. Features very Negroid and ugly. Mosquitos. At night when the moon rose heard shouts and drumming in distant villages. Passed a bad night. (*Congo Diary*, 9)

One sees little sign in these diary entries of the powerful, poetic novel that was to be born from his experiences in the Congo, or of the consciousness of the man who wrote it. *Heart of Darkness* was hailed by Cunninghame Graham, John Galsworthy, and Arthur Conan Doyle as a powerful and radical assault against imperialism. Yet, newly returned to London in February 1891, when he surely was aware that administrators representing King Leopold in the Congo—no less than agents of private firms like the SAB—were all engaged in piracy and murder, Conrad "demonstrated interest, incredibly, in returning to Africa if he could obtain command of one of the steamers run by the Prince Steam Shipping Co. of Antwerp" (Karl 1979, 310–11).

Conrad's indictment of imperialism in *Heart of Darkness* is not unequivocal. The angry voice of dissent is subverted by a symbolism inherently racist, and in *Lord Jim,* which he started before and completed after *Heart of Darkness,* there are several ringing tributes to the spirit and legacy of the imperial mission. A prevailing nineteenth-century cultural myth is probably responsible for his ambivalence.

Imperialism was presented and seen as a noble, disinterested impulse to "civilize" and "raise the spiritual and intellectual consciousness of" the "backward" peoples of the earth. Thomas Carlyle eloquently argued that it was the mission—indeed, moral duty—of the Anglo-Saxon race to bring the riches of its culture to primitive peoples. Christianity gave sanction to this idea of bringing religion, hygiene, and "light" to people degraded by their backwardness and ignorance of God. The myth of the imperial mission was further promulgated by social Darwinists, who based their interpretation of the development of human society on Darwin's discoveries of the biological laws of animal and plant life, and by Herbert Spencer's evolutionary theory, which he derived from Darwin. Spencer's application of the laws of natural selection, which he called survival of the fittest, encouraged the competitiveness of nations, and validated European colonial expansion. By dominating other peoples, European nations "proved" that they were the fittest to survive. The proliferation of their culture was an essential step "towards a higher form of human organisation" (Watt 1979, 156), and the means whereby all humanity would ascend the evolutionary ladder. That white races were dominant was itself the result of inherited superiority. Benjamin Kidd in *The Control of the Tropics* (1898) carried the ideology a step further. He defended the domination and destruction of inferior races as a necessary stage in the evolutionary process. The implicit assumption, hardly to be questioned, was that primitive peoples, being so much less evolved, were not very many notches above man's animal antecedents.

The newly democratized masses, to the drum of the popular press, were fervent in their nationalism and patriotism; and, at least in England, they were feverish in their support of imperialist and racist ideology. Imperialism was a "larger patriotism," a way of maintaining one's national prestige. The *Daily Mail* (established in 1896) built a readership of one million strong to the tattoo of its manifesto: "to the power, supremacy, and greatness of the British Empire." A series of imperialist books stressing the indigenous virtue and superiority of the English became runaway best-sellers—Charles Dilke's *Greater Britain* (1869), John Robert Seeley's *The Expansion of England* (1883), and James Anthony Froude's *Oceana, or England and Her Colonies* (1886). The British public gobbled them up as tributes to the common Englishman, who shook his fist at a united Germany. Kipling and H. Rider Haggard were enormously popular. Their novels, set in exotic parts of the empire, fulfilled industrial workers' yearning for adventure, and enacted their fantasies. The heroes in these outposts of progress were always white and never afraid to be masterful. Robert Louis Stevenson's tales of savages, and Father Ohrwalder's *Ten Years' Captivity in the Mahdi's Camp* (1892) likewise fostered popular racist misconceptions. George W. Steevens's *With Kitchener to Khartum* ran to thirteen editions in 1898, the year Conrad began writing *Heart of Darkness*.

It is no wonder, in this virulently proimperialist climate, that the novel's indictment should be scarred by the unconscious imprint of a prevailing cultural myth—and by what Conrad had actually done and felt as a colonizer.

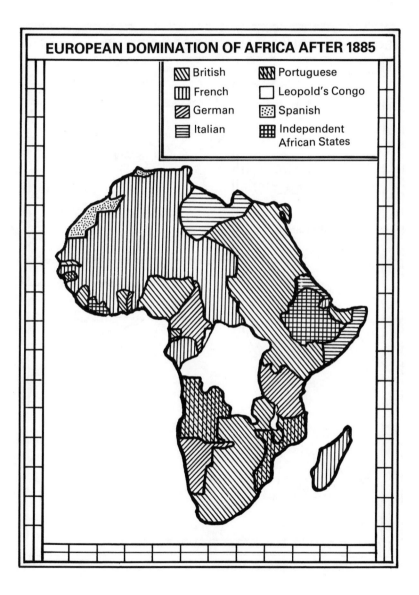

EUROPEAN DOMINATION OF AFRICA AFTER 1885

British
French
German
Italian
Portuguese
Leopold's Congo
Spanish
Independent African States

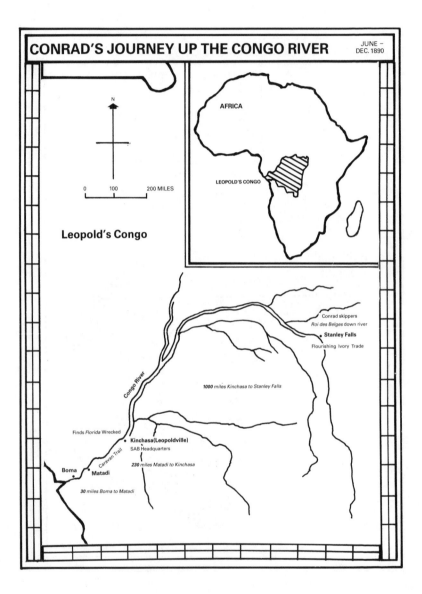

CONRAD'S JOURNEY UP THE CONGO RIVER

JUNE – DEC. 1890

N

0   100   200 MILES

Leopold's Congo

AFRICA

LEOPOLD'S CONGO

Conrad skippers
Roi des Belges down river
● **Stanley Falls**
Flourishing Ivory Trade

1000 miles Kinchasa to Stanley Falls

Congo River

Finds *Florida* Wrecked
● **Kinchasa(Leopoldville)**
SAB Headquarters
Caravan Trail
230 miles Matadi to Kinchasa

Boma ● **Matadi**

30 miles Boma to Matadi

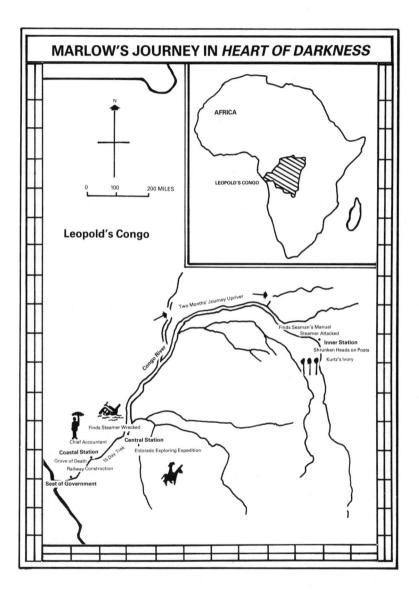

MARLOW'S JOURNEY IN *HEART OF DARKNESS*

N

0   100   200 MILES

Leopold's Congo

AFRICA

LEOPOLD'S CONGO

Two Months' Journey Upriver

Finds Seaman's Manual
Steamer Attacked

Inner Station
Shrunken Heads on Posts

Kurtz's Ivory

Congo River

Finds Steamer Wrecked

Chief Accountant

Central Station
Eldorado Exploring Expedition

Coastal Station

15 Day Trek

Grove of Death

Railway Construction

Seat of Government

45

V

A Reading of the Text

Introduction: Frame Story, Themes, Meaning of Psychic Encounter

Eight years after his colonial experience in the Congo, Conrad wrote *Heart of Darkness*. In the summer of 1898, he had written a short story, "Youth," about his adventures as second mate of the *Palestine*, which freighted coal to the Far East, and had adopted a persona—Marlow—as his first-person narrator. The Marlow of *Heart of Darkness* is also the narrator of an adventure that Conrad himself experienced but had never quite understood. Marlow's story is Conrad's own coming to terms with his traumatic experience in the Belgian Congo when he felt a vicious, self-serving hatred for the people exploited there. Ultimately he learned from his own trauma, from the shattering of his naive political consciousness, to recognize in himself the behavior of the classic, reprehensible European colonizer. The story proper is Marlow's monologue: so subtle in its depiction of an individual's struggle against losing moral identity as seemingly to bear the unconscious imprint of the trauma it records. At the same time, it is a tour de force remarkably musical in the range and variety of thought and emotion expressed by a single voice. This monologue is given a frame that establishes a setting for the narrative—Marlow and his friends aboard the sailing yawl *Nellie*, anchored on the river Thames, waiting for the evening tide. The frame story also functions as a means for delineating the character of Marlow the narrator, and does so by anticipating his narrative. The telling twist to this preparation is that the anticipated speech is not the one that is given.

The preparation amounts to this: his story is about the operations—that is, piracy and murder—of a European company's trade in Africa, and Marlow's English friends, his *Nellie* audience, are all company men—a director of companies, a Tory lawyer, an accountant—who are playing a game of dominoes, "toying . . . with the bones" (3).[6] In the context of the story Marlow is to tell, the company men's toying with bones carries a resonance—tusks of ivory, bones of Africa—that anticipates the horrors Marlow is to describe in his story. The platform onto which Marlow steps, Conrad's frame story—his select English audience, a great riverway, a "brooding gloom" over London, against which one of them raises a tribute to the empire—appears to be specifically designed to implicate the English in a wholesale indictment of imperialism. Marlow, however, does not give the prepared speech; as it turns out, his intention is to exclude the English from criticism. " 'And this also,' said Marlow suddenly, 'has been one of the dark places of the earth' " (5). What he begins talking about—England of the Roman era—undercuts the reader's expectation of an attack on imperialism. While darkness has been associated with imperialism through the gloom over London, the shroud of which extends to the far corners of the earth, suddenly these associations are reversed; darkness is identified with primitive peoples, with the wilderness, with, by implication, the vast regions of the earth brought into the light by the civilizing mission. It is as if Marlow were giving the wrong speech at a political rally.

This surprising twist, which is the prelude to excluding his listeners and nation from criticism, piques one's interest in Marlow, who sits cross-legged like a Buddha against the mizzenmast. The reader learns that Marlow's state of "enlightenment" prevents him from making wholesale indictments. His story not only tells what he saw in colonial Africa, but also discloses the unconscious motive of his compulsion to go, and remain. He had been hardly more than an unthinking animal, and—if self-induced naïveté can be called innocence—innocent when he journeyed to the Congo. The truths about himself and the world are revealed symbolically by the significance of the journey to Kurtz as a journey from civilized inhibition into knowledge of the darkness, of the death wish, away from the constraints of the civilized ego. In *Civilization and Its Discontents,* Freud develops the idea that normal aggressive instincts are internalized and transformed under the pressure of civilizing restraints into guilt, suppressed violence, and a corresponding death wish. Aggressive instincts are normal; civilization perverts them. Marlow is driven by this unconscious psychology, kicking and posturing all the way, to a meeting with a man who is the mirror image of himself unfettered by inhibitions. From the shock of this psychic encounter with his unacknowledged self he learns, for one thing, that the true motive of the imperial mission is the same as his unconscious motive for having gone to Africa. Africa appealed to an inner need to open the throttle for a nihilistic joy ride, and so vent a little of the darkness within. Marlow implies by his story that this destructive urge underlies the compulsion that has made colonizers of him and his fellow Europeans.

As he begins his story, two intolerable truths undercut and neutralize the anger of his indictment of imperialism. One is the cynical vision he has acquired—that the subjugation of Africa is part of the tragic price paid for civilization. The other, and deeper source of his pessimism, derives from the horrifying trauma he experienced in his struggle against losing control. Marlow has had firsthand experience of what happens to men freed of civilizing restraints; of how, having no rationale other than conquest and plunder, their savagery becomes inseparable from the wilderness in which it finds license, and they go mad, either dementedly grubbing like insects or worshiping their own omnipotence. In retrospect, he is left affirming the necessity of civilization and its restraints. In doing so, he also resigns himself to what he sees as the inevitable product of civilization: imperialism.

The Congo has made a different man of Marlow, one adept at valuing small distinctions, such as discriminating between the lesser of evils in judging his fellow creatures. He is not capable of making a wholesale attack on imperialism. He can only, in his "enlightened" state, make one of his fine distinctions—so fine as to be rendered invalid by the truth his story discloses. Marlow's spiritual state is epitomized by Lear's reflection, "[n]ot being the worst / Stands in some rank of praise" (*King Lear* 2. 4. 251–52); for it is thus, beset like the old king with only different grades of wickedness to choose among, that he declares the imperialism of England to be virtuous when compared to that of its Continental competitors. He draws an analogy between his own experience of breakdown in the Congo and that of a young Roman colonizer in the wilderness of England nineteen hundred years before. Rome's mission, like that of the Continental powers—but without their pretense—was piracy. Marlow pictures for his *Nellie* audience the decent young citizen in a toga who comes to Britain ostensibly to mend his fortunes, who breaks down in stages— "the growing regrets, the longing to escape, the powerless disgust, the surrender, the hate" (6). Conrad's sympathy is predominantly with the fate of the colonizer. The Roman in the toga loses control and becomes savage just as did the Belgian Kurtz, and quite nearly the Englishman Marlow himself, in Belgian colonial Africa. By contrast, Marlow implies, this sort of madness and savagery is less likely to occur where the Union Jack waves; more of the good things of civilization are likely to be bestowed upon the Africans by the English, because they are able to organize an administration predicated upon an ideal, and to run it efficiently.

One can see in the narrator the sensibilities of a man who has learned to accept the status quo and stop fighting it. The realities, or truths he has learned about himself, about imperial Europe, about the meaning of all values—truths that ultimately require his political suicide and allegiance to the values of the English imperialist—are symbolized by his face-to-face meeting with the first-class agent Kurtz. The narrator's story is an evocatively intimate record of the naive Marlow's struggle to know and yet not to know the unacknowledged Kurtz within himself. Marlow seems to be caught in a spell: under a strange compulsion that has him venturing to Africa and perservering against every obstacle, regardless of the cost to his own soul and sanity, while on a conscious level he is struggling against the slippery moral evasiveness of his behavior. What should we make of his expressions of moral indignation, and the registerings of his disgust for the other colonizers, implied by his sarcasm and irony? What should we make of his testimonies to duty, to backbreaking devotion to the work at hand as a staff against temptation and a brace supporting fidelity to standards of decency? How should we take his repeated emphasis upon the virtue of restraint, described in *Lord Jim* as "an unthinking and blessed stiffness before the outward and inward terrors, before the might of nature, and the seductive corruption of men"[7] when he remains in a compromised situation? Kurtz makes Marlow see himself as an imposter. The sum of all the truths Marlow is to learn is symbolized by this encounter, which leaves him unmasked and incapable of resisting the suspicion of having indulged in Kurtz's terrible freedom.

Marlow, under the charm of the snake (the Congo "fascinated me as a snake would a bird—a silly little bird" [8]) is driven to Kurtz in the half-delirium of uncontrollable emotions—fear (the discovery that he does not have the will to turn back); hate (the temptation to act as if anything were permissible); and terror (the recoiling from the thrill of letting go of one's controls and falling off a precipice).

It is a distinctive feature of the novel that as Marlow approaches his meeting with Kurtz and the psychic pressure mounts, his defense mechanisms take on ideological significance. A symbolism emerges— the Africans and the wilderness as degenerative influences, the journey to the interior of Africa as regression to savagery—that appears to undercut the dominant, anti-imperialist theme of the novel. Much critical debate has been generated by the problem of how to interpret the inherently racist implications of this symbolism, which serves to excuse the colonizer by blaming the Africans for the behavior of the Europeans. It must be stressed, however, that the political reality of the novel is seen through the sensibilities of an individual undergoing moral collapse, and the chief symptom of this collapse is the distorted view we are given of Africans. Marlow, in his efforts to maintain a moral posture, while unconsciously pandering to the instinctual lusts that brought him to Africa in the first place, begins to hate and blame the exploited people themselves. It is the last and most desperate of his self-exculpating strategies, and it collapses when he meets Kurtz.

In addition to *Heart of Darkness*, both *Lord Jim* and "The Secret Sharer" describe what happens to a central character brought face to face with his double. In each work, the encounter with the double has a different effect and implicit value. One is ambiguous; one enhances moral growth; and the third deepens pessimism and despair. Jim's double—the shadow-terror from which he has been in flight since his dereliction of duty as a ship's officer—is a man he fears he will become if he admits his cowardice. When the dreaded event occurs, he meets a man of intense egoism, vengefully ruthless, with a righteous grievance against the world. Brown, like Kurtz and the murderer Leggatt of "The Secret Sharer," is the dark power in the hero's psyche—the embodiment of his particular potential for evil, as Hyde is Jekyll's unacknowledged alter ego. The spiritual drama in these stories lies in the hero's relationship to his unacknowledged self. The encounter in each case is made to appear inevitable. Jim, in abandoning his post on the *Patna* when it collides with a submerged wreck, should be seen as encountering his own inner necessity. He has been dreaming his life away, blind to reality, seeking the easier berth. When the collision occurs, it is as if it represents the impulse within Jim's psyche to destroy himself—destroy, that is, the idealized conception of his personality that had made a prisoner of him. The test implicit in this moment of reckoning for Jim is whether or not he has the courage to face himself after he jumps.

These encounters represent a face-to-face meeting with one's worst fears, and are potentially liberating. For, if the hero passes the test, there is the chance of his emerging stronger and less guilt-ridden. In *Lord Jim*, for example, the trial could have had the positive effect of making Jim less guarded, less committed to his own idealized version of himself.

The actions described in *Lord Jim*, "The Secret Sharer," and *Heart of Darkness* reflect psychic as well as real events—objective circumstances that reveal the hero to himself. Such epiphanies, which Dorothy van Ghent calls "['showings'] from the daemonic underground of the psyche" (1953, 240), have unambiguously positive value in "The Secret Sharer."

> The captain in "The Secret Sharer" acknowledges his profound kinship with a man who has violently transgressed the captain's professional code (the man has murdered another seaman during

a voyage, and murder at sea is, in Conrad, something worse than murder; whatever its excuses, it is an inexcusable breach of faith with a community bound together by common hazard); but by the acknowledgment he masters his own identity, integrates, as it were, his unconscious impulses within consciousness, and thereby realizes self-command and command of his ship. (233)

The captain's sharing of Leggatt's guilt destroys the idealized self he projects to conceal latent insecurity, and so transforms his personality by making him more conscious of his moral existence. By contrast, in both *Lord Jim* and *Heart of Darkness,* Conrad is ambivalent about the value of such intimate self-disclosure. Jim, as a result of the *Patna* incident, becomes passionately committed to his idealized perception of self. Haunted by suspicions of inadequacy against which he struggles to defend himself, he is inspired to greatness in Patusan. It can be argued that Jim is responsible for the catastrophe there, which occurs on account of his self-delusions. But one might as convincingly contend that he followed his dream and shaped the world by his example, much like Don Quixote.

Similarly, Marlow, in *Heart of Darkness,* offers no clear-cut illustration of the value of facing the truth about himself. Like the captain in "The Secret Sharer," he too becomes intimately involved with his double, but is deeply disturbed by the experience. The character who emerges after the shattering of Marlow's idealized self is like Gulliver after his voyage to the Houyhnhnms: contemptuous of so-called civilized people. *Heart of Darkness,* in contrast to "The Secret Sharer," is a dark meditation on the problem of evil. Truth in "The Secret Sharer" reinforces the captain's faith in the code he practices. Truth in *Heart of Darkness* calls into question the whole store of civilizing restraints—work, duty, Christianity—and the meaning of all values. Conrad's novel poses fundamental questions. Is Marlow, at the end, left at a crossroads in his life where all directions lead to moral annihilation? Or does his experience, by promoting a greater understanding of human destructive tendencies, encourage faith in "the modest countertruths on which civilisation depends" (Watt 1979, 167)?

Heart of Darkness works simultaneously on the three levels of politics, metaphysics, and psychology. It addresses itself to Europe's exploitation of Africa, to the problem of evil, and to the pressure of psychic need upon the resistance of personality. Self-knowledge, though it may expose a powerful death wish, is potentially liberating. But what is the truth that ultimately emerges from Marlow's experience? Is it the ugly truth about imperialism? Or is it a tainted version of that truth—an indictment neutralized by Conrad's own ambivalence, by a self-exculpating metaphysical conception within which the indictment is contained, and by the "scarring," as Anne McClintock argues, of the undoubtedly racist depiction of Africans (1984, 52)? Is the novel to be regarded as a parable suggesting that people are vicious, weak, and thankless, and that therefore it is always a victory when they find the means to subjugate themselves? Or is the truth rather that they have been bound too tightly in the mummy cloth of social restraints? Have civilized people become, consequently, vicious savages wearing masks of moral superiority? In choosing between two alternatives, to dominate or to be destroyed, must they inevitably self-destruct? What then is the psychological effect of the experience? Does self-knowledge promote a more humanely conscious, moral existence? Does it germinate into religious faith? Or does it deepen pessimism and darken despair?

Through the Portals

Marlow gets his command of a Congo steamboat through the patronage of his well-connected aunt, and the sudden, strange death of one of the trading company's captains: "a couple of years already out there engaged in the noble cause, you know, and he probably felt the need at last of asserting his self-respect in some way" (9). The point of this affair—Marlow is to be stepping into Fresleven's shoes—is to underscore the odds against the new recruit. The dead captain, this "gentlest, quietest creature" (9) beat a village chief with a stick because of an altercation over two black hens, and was speared through the back by the chief's son. Three years of "the noble cause" have done him in. *"Du calme,"* Marlow is advised by the company doctor, who is convinced that anybody going to Africa must be crazy. This doctor, an absurd, "unshaven little man in a thread-bare coat like a gaberdine, with his feet in slippers" (11), asks if he might measure Marlow's head. " 'I always ask leave, in the interests of science, to measure the crania of those going out there,' he said. 'And when they come back too?' I asked. 'Oh, I never see them,' he remarked; 'and, moreover, the changes take place inside, you know' " (11).

Almost everything Marlow describes has this "touch of insanity" about it, as if he were the straight man in a farce that becomes increasingly desperate as he enters upon its stage. His experience in Africa is a nightmare farce about a straight man struggling in desperate earnestness to maintain his sense of identity. One gathers that Marlow's predecessor, Captain Fresleven, like the decent young Roman in a toga, broke down from an intolerable sense of his own powerlessness to suppress the passions invariably awakened in colonial environments.

Because the novel is a symbolic account of a Westerner's descent into the darkness of an alien culture, the darkness within his own civilized ego, and the darkness of imperialistic brutality, one is impelled to ask whether Conrad modeled its structure on one of the traditional epic descents into the underworld. Robert O. Evans, for instance, attempts to show that the novel "resembles a skeletalized version of the *Inferno*" (1956, 58).[8] For the most part, such analyses are unconvincing. The exception is Lillian Feder's essay, in which she argues that Conrad made calculated use of the sixth book of the *Aeneid*. Feder makes no claim for close modeling, but rather underlines essential similarities born out of the myth itself. Marlow, for instance, is like Aeneas in that he explores, by means of his journey, "the depths of his own and his nation's conscience." Like Aeneas, he learns "of the bloodshed and cruelty which are to weigh on the conscience of his nation"—the cost of imperial power, Rome's and Europe's (1955, 280, 281).

But all in all, *Heart of Darkness* resembles traditional accounts of the hero's descent to the underworld only in the most general sense.

Marlow's story begins at the company's offices where he signs his contract, and climaxes when he meets his unacknowledged self. At the end of his journey, he is left with a confirmation of his shame and guilt—his moral failing for having remained in the company's employment. The fact of his remaining is like the fact of Jim's jumping from the *Patna;* Marlow's story is an explanation of, an accounting for, this damning fact. But Conrad, through strategies of the narrative, presents Marlow's guilt, like Jim's, in an equivocal light. Marlow's guilt is made to seem but a small fact, and altogether inevitable in the greater picture. For beyond the question of individual or even collective responsibility, Marlow's accounting for his moral failing is contained by a metaphysical conception that dismisses moral considerations from the world of the novel: it is the idea of God (or fate) as a cosmic knitting machine indifferently stitching individuals in and out in patterns regulated by the inalterable laws of historical necessity. In a letter of December 1897, Conrad bitterly reacts to what he takes to be naive moralizing from his socialist admirer. Fate, he tells Cunninghame Graham, is a cosmic knitting machine "that . . . [has] made itself without thought, without conscience, without foresight, without eyes, without heart. It is a tragic accident—and it has happened. You can't interfere with it. The last drop of bitterness is in the suspicion that you can't even smash it. . . . It knits us in and it knits us out. It has knitted time space, pain, death, corruption, despair and all the illusions—and nothing matters. I'll admit however that to look at the remorseless process is sometimes amusing" (Watts 1969, 56–57).

This attitude toward fate is suggested in both *Heart of Darkness* and *Lord Jim* by a similar device at the beginning of the hero's confession. In *Heart of Darkness* it is symbolized by the two women Marlow meets at the company offices, one fat, the other slim, "knitting black wool" before the portals through which he was to step to the encounter with his destiny. Who, after all, are these black knitters ushering him through the portals toward participation in the raping of a continent, but obvious representatives of fate? Symbolically, they stand at the doors of the repressed life. Literally, they funnel repressed violence into an imperialist outlet. Marlow is only, after all, a victim of inalterable laws—merely an atom in the pressure cooker of Western civilization. His invocation of the fates—while he is on the threshold of telling a story about his reprehensible behavior in Africa—is self-defensive rationalization. In this respect Marlow and Conrad are alike, for this self-defensive rationalization is part of the poetic vision of the novel. Frederick Crews has observed that Conrad's "engagement in his plots would seem to have more to do with self-exculpation than with dispassionate analysis" (1967, 514).[9]

Before embarking for Africa, Marlow visits with his aunt who obtained the command for him, and who, in a triumphant mood, exults about his mission of "weaning those ignorant millions from their horrid ways" (12). Her excessive zeal upsets him. He was no less zealous in using her to obtain the command, but what *were* his motives? "A queer feeling came to me that I was an imposter" (13), he says. But he was a missionary in the eyes of his aunt, and presented as a gifted being to the company. He is startled to note that he feels uneasy about this venture, and that his casual attitude seems like affectation.

The Journey

To the Coastal Station.   The voyage on a French steamer down the west coast of Africa (Bordeaux to Boma, at the mouth of the Congo) is the first leg of a journey to the heart of "a mournful and senseless delusion" (13)—*la mission civilisatrice*. Marlow feels an eerie foreboding. What he sees of French efforts to make headway against an immense jungle continent—with settlements scattered like pinheads—is fantastic and sordid, and yet he cannot, will not commit himself to oppose the colonial enterprise. He wonders whether he is dreaming. Occasional meetings with a boat full of Africans shouting, singing, streaming with perspiration momentarily break the spell. There was nothing phantomlike about them, and "they wanted no excuse for being there" (14). The most striking hallucinatory experience is of a French man-of-war shelling the coast: like a toy, with the muzzles of her six-inch guns sticking out over the hull, her ensign limp in the steaming heat. Pop, pop would go her guns. There was not even a shed there, yet men in the warboat "were dying of fever at the rate of three a day" (14). "Lugubrious drollery," "touch of insanity," "merry dance of death and trade": such expressions represent Marlow's effort at defining himself in a nightmarish place, like an "overheated catacomb" (14). It takes the ship more than thirty days to reach the mouth of the big river.

On the passage to the first of the company's three stations (at Matadi), the morose captain of the river steamer expresses an attitude toward the agents of trade that anticipates Marlow's own: he is angrily contemptuous, and sardonic—betrayed by the influence of the place into pitying himself. This same split in Marlow—between the capacity for moral judgment, and the fear of losing control—is characteristic of the breakdown that even the most civilized Europeans suffered in colonial environments. For Marlow's struggle against losing control is like that of a man squirming for footing on quicksand—a foregone conclusion—because no amount of moral posturing can cover the condemning fact of his staying on as agent of the company. Gradually, his identity as a member of the civilized community must be lost. Imperceptibly, he comes to hate everything about the alien world, including the suffering Africans, as if the country and the people caused the corruption rather than being innocent victims of it. Despite his compassion for the Africans, Marlow, as he enters the interior, comes perilously close to the mad rage that brought Fresleven's career to an end.

At first sight, through the continuous noise of rapids and glare of sunlight, the company station appears to be a mirage of "inhabited devastation" (15). Marlow makes out three wooden, barracklike structures on a rocky slope; numbers of people, mostly black and naked, moving about like ants; a waste of excavations; and a jetty projecting into the river. Then, on the path to the company office, he "[comes] upon a boiler wallowing in the grass," a "railway truck lying . . . on its back with its wheels in the air" (16), and decaying machinery—the peculiar evidence of a railroad under construction. Marlow is impressed by what appears to be "objectless blasting" (16).

Establishing the historical context of the novel, Hunt Hawkins writes that work on the railway from this first station at Matadi up to the Central Station at Kinshasa began in March 1890, three months before Conrad arrived in the country. The 270 miles of line was needed to bypass cataracts separating the lower from the upper river with its 7,000-mile system of navigable waterways. With the railway, the rubber, ivory, and vegetable products of the interior could be transported profitably to the coast. Thus the line became the one major capital improvement that Leopold attempted during his rule (Hawkins 1979, 290).

A merry farce with a touch of insanity? A work gang of Africans six in a file, each one spiritless and starving, and linked one to the other by an iron collar, go clanking by, balancing small baskets of earth on their heads; Marlow is saluted by a rascally, grinning soldier put in charge of these "criminals." Although in the Berlin Conference, Leopold pledged to "improve the moral well-being of the inhabitants of the Congo," he instead enslaved them by imposing forced labor, and by impressing less tractable Africans into chain gangs. Forced labor on a small scale began the year Conrad was in the Congo. On 9 August 1890, "a royal decree permitted the railway company to establish a militia to impress workers from the surrounding area" (Hawkins 1979, 292). Leopold's apologists such as Baron Moncheur, the Belgian minister in Washington, brazenly justified these policies, claiming that they were "a distinctly civilizing influence," teaching the Africans habits of industry, and thus setting them on the road to civilization (Hawkins 1979, 292). Though appalled by the suggestion that he also was "a part of the great cause of these high and just proceedings" (16), Marlow does not think of turning back. He bestirs himself, passes a large, quarry-sized hole, dug there for no reason he can discern, but possibly out of a philanthropic desire to teach the natives the habit of industry, and takes cover from the sun under some trees. His retreat turns out to be the place where the workers come to die. "Brought from all the recesses of the coast in all the legality of time contracts, lost in uncongenial surroundings, fed on unfamiliar food, they sickened, became inefficient, and were then allowed to crawl away and rest" (17). It is estimated that more than three million Africans died in this way during the last fifteen years of Leopold's rule.

Marlow gives one of the dying men a biscuit:

> . . . glancing down, I saw a face near my hand. The black bones reclined at full length with one shoulder against the tree, and slowly the eyelids rose and the sunken eyes looked up at me, enormous and vacant, a kind of blind, white flicker in the depths of the orbs, which died out slowly. The man seemed young—almost a boy—but you know with them it's hard to tell. I found nothing else to do but to offer him one of my good Swede's ship's biscuits I had in my pocket. The fingers closed slowly on it and held— there was no other movement and no other glance. (17–18)

The horror communicated by this little episode probably inspired the reformers who eventually ended Leopold's rule. In October 1909, E. D. Morel, head of the Congo Reform Association, wrote Arthur Conan Doyle, one of its members, "that Conrad's story was the 'most powerful work ever written on the subject'" (Hawkins 1979, 293). Marlow continues, "While I stood horror-struck, one of these creatures rose to his hands and knees, and went off on all-fours towards the river to drink. He lapped out of his hand, then sat up in the sunlight, crossing his shins in front of him, and after a time let his woolly head fall on his breastbone" (18).

In revulsion, Marlow hastens away from the grove toward the station, and runs into the company's chief accountant, a man with brushed hair and starched collar, immaculately groomed, and toting a green parasol. He had come out from his bookkeeping chores "to get a breath of fresh air" (18).

Can Marlow have missed the callousness of such a remark? He can hardly have missed it, but is so entirely preoccupied with the problem of his own survival—how to be, to conform to what, to side with whom in this ungodly place—that he goes overboard in his response to what he takes to be the man's significance for him. "In the great demoralisation of the land he kept up his appearance. That's backbone. . . . And he was devoted to his books, which were in apple-pie order" (18).

What Marlow responds to instinctively in this keeping up of appearances is a sense of the man's inner reserve, of capacity for fidelity, even if it be to the starched, white collars of his shirts. The fundamental question of how Marlow can remain in the service of the company is altogether sidestepped. He is unwilling to confront the horrors around him; his sole concern is to maintain a posture of moral superiority, while staying on as a company man. Marlow, having discovered that as an employee of the company he is aiding and abetting murder, ought promptly to have resigned his appointment. He does not break his contract, and fails to take a moral stand, because he is pursuing the unconscious motive that brought him to Africa in the first place. His respect for the chief agent is not an expression of grudging admiration, but of gratitude. By Jove, one can survive! Immediately, there is a change in Marlow, a thickening of the skin, and he begins to use the word *nigger,* commonplace enough at the time, consistently. His equilibrium depends upon his being less appalled.

During the ten days he is at the station, he idles his time away sitting on the floor in the accountant's office, while the chief agent, slightly scented and perched on a high stool, writes in his ledger books, keeping minute account of the "rubbishy" goods carried upcountry by caravan, and the crate loads of precious material shipped from his station to the home office; or complains about the distracting groans of a dying agent put on a truckle bed in the office. The man is chillingly indifferent to everything but his books and the prodigies of an agent a thousand miles upriver in ivory country who is more productive than all the agents of the company put together, and destined to be "a somebody in the Administration before long" (20). Marlow makes no moral judgment, even when the fellow, in exasperation at having been disturbed by the arrival of a caravan of porters, professes " . . . to hate those savages—hate them to the death" (19). Marlow quietly registers the fantastic callousness of the man. He remains a passive employee given to irony and increasingly fascinated by the idea of meeting the remarkable agent working the interior so productively. The idea of meeting Kurtz, and the compulsion to get to his outpost, is to become in Marlow's mind his justification for continuing on his journey.

In explaining Marlow's behavior, critics have generally looked at the question historically, considering Conrad as a product of his time. To paraphrase Hesse, he was a microcosm of the tragedy of his age; and seen in the context of the times, Marlow might be thought unusually independent, even enlightened. One must recognize the forces that predisposed Conrad to sympathize with colonial policies. He felt a debt of obligation to the English—the Polish refugee become naturalized citizen—which was strengthened by his hatred of Germany—one of the three nations that had partitioned his homeland, and one of England's competitors in the "scramble for Africa." Furthermore, because of his deep fear of betraying trust, and his genuine belief that true liberty was possible only under the English flag, he encouraged patriotic support of English policy, which meant support of imperialism. Finally, his story was intended to appear as a serial in the conservative *Blackwood's Magazine*.[10] Considering these facts, one might conclude that Conrad was remarkable to have been as independent in his thinking as he was. In any case, the argument continues in his defense: like Conrad, Marlow was out there as an explorer, not as a colonizer.

These explanations appear irrelevant when one understands Marlow's behavior as a symptom of his struggle against his own destructive instinct. His moral equivocation is the first stage in a hopeless effort to maintain a moral posture and at the same time to remain in the employ of the company. The story uncovers the unconscious motive of the imperial mission, and presents a drama of moral collapse. Marlow discovers in Kurtz his mirror image, the image of himself as he would be if he were unfettered by inhibitions: the great, white colonizer.

To the Central Station.   To get to his steamboat, Marlow makes a two-hundred-mile, overland trek by caravan to the Central Station, at which point the river becomes navigable for eight hundred miles of upriver trade, to Kurtz's outpost. The region between the two stations was depopulated when the Bangala fled to avoid forced labor. Marlow describes a great monotony of paths, grass, hills, heat, occasional abandoned villages, with few incidents occurring during the fifteen days before he hobbles into the Central Station. He is beginning to see how easy it is to become unhinged in the Congo. Everything is permissible; everything is irritating. Critics especially interested in the political dimension of the novel, like John A. McClure in his study of Kipling and Conrad, see *Heart of Darkness* as a classic illustration of the drastic personality changes Europeans typically experienced in colonial environments. McClure lists the dangers to self-control: "the terrible monotony of the life, the claustrophobic isolation, the physical discomfort, the inefficiency and breakdowns inevitable in a situation where the master is an ignorant alien and his servants, virtually slaves, have little incentive but fear to obey orders" (1981, 134). Marlow has good reason to remember the company's eccentric doctor who thought people who take such risks must be driven by powerful irrational impulses.

At the Central Station, which is on a backwater bordered by a mudbank, a forest, and a dilapidated fence of rushes, Marlow discovers that his steamer is at the bottom of the river. He suspects that the manager of the station, jealous of Kurtz and wishing him dead, deliberately had it wrecked. Two days before Marlow's arrival they "had started . . . in a sudden hurry up the river with the manager on board, in charge of some volunteer skipper," and fairly promptly "tore the bottom out of her on stones" (21). She sank adjacent to the confines of the station. Marlow learns that Kurtz is rumored to be ill, and later will see the wrecking of the steamboat as an attempt to assure his death. But he cannot be certain of anything in such an environment. It is altogether too incredible; he feels as if he is among phantoms with long staves, gliding hither and yon between the confines of a rotting fence, breathing and murmuring incessantly of ivory.[11] The manager is a man devoid of administrative ability, learning, and intelligence. What he does have is indomitable health, possibly because there is nothing in him to take sick. At any rate, he has a heroic constitution and no conscience.

Marlow, feeling exceedingly uneasy about his reasons for staying on, pounces on the immediate problem of rescuing his steamer from the river. The nasty business of dredging up the wreck and repairing it, he tells his *Nellie* audience, was at any rate "real" work, and real work of any sort in this infernal place was what a man needed to "keep [his] hold on the redeeming facts of life" (23). Of course his work will reclaim the steamer for the service of the trade; and work, on the symbolic level—the restoration of the means of getting to Kurtz—secretly furthers the unconscious desire that brought him to colonial Africa. Marlow turns his back on the agents of the station, throwing himself day and night into the salvage of his riverboat. He despises the pilgrims of the trade with a biting sarcasm. Their depravity is a gauge by which he measures his own moral health. Part of Marlow's instinctive strategy, by which he presumes himself to be morally superior to the other agents, is to exaggerate the senseless and bizarre behavior of his fellow colonizers.

A shed filled with the trash used in barter with natives bursts into flame. A stout man rushes to the river with a tin pail, gathers about a quart of water, and hurries back to the fire. Marlow notices that there is a hole in the bottom of the pail. An African worker is beaten. The brickmaster at the station, the manager's favorite, has done nothing for a year because whatever he needed to make bricks, straw possibly, could not be found there. One suspects that what Marlow describes here is exaggerated in order to make his own posture look sane by contrast. The reality of the station may be ugly and morally compromising, but certainly not quite so lunatic.

The danger to Marlow, as McClure sees it (referring to Octave Mannoni's study of the colonial experience in Madagascar), is that "the sudden social decompression" will make him " 'blow up' emotionally," and become like his fellow colonizers who

> bully, beat, and even kill the Africans on the slightest pretext, and their ability so to dominate another people causes their egos to inflate grotesquely, until they see themselves as gods. With this development the situation takes on a vicious sort of stability, for

as gods the Europeans no longer feel bound by human moral codes, nor do they see their domination of the Africans as unnatural. Moreover, as humans playing gods, they enjoy reaffirming their new and shaky status by frequent exercises of arbitrary absolutism. . . . But the stability of the colonial situation is only temporary. The pilgrims, blinded by their sense of infinite superiority, succumb to flabbiness and inefficiency. . . . All are corrupted by an environment they thought they had overcome. (1981, 142–43)

Marlow is perhaps somewhat less threatened by this pathology because he is not acquisitive. But this is a small reservation. He is white, morally compromised, and in an alien environment; and the extent to which he is threatened can be seen in his increasing fear of losing control. The longer he is in Africa, and the nearer he is to his meeting with Kurtz, the shakier he feels, and the more the wilderness appears to him a threatening, degrading place. Marlow's breaking point is anticipated as the identification between him and Kurtz is intensified.

Conrad contrives to tighten that identification by involving Marlow in the manager's intrigues, and in the jealous fears of the manager's *protégé* the brickmaker, whose hopes of becoming assistant manager have been dashed by the arrival of Kurtz. The remarkable Kurtz had bypassed the usual ladder of advancement in the trade, and had received by special dispensation first-class agent status in the heart of ivory country; but for some reason the brickmaker thinks Kurtz will upset his plans for becoming a measly assistant manager. A "*papier-mâché* Mephistopheles" (26), he actually pumps Marlow for information, believing him to be, like Kurtz, one of those destined to make it to the top. What makes him think so is the language used in the home office communiqué on Fresleven's replacement, which describes the new captain as having come out "for the guidance of the cause entrusted to us by Europe" (25–26), and unmistakably recalls the voice of the eloquent Kurtz. Nor is the brickmaker mistaken in thinking that "the same people who sent him specially also recommended you" (26); for who else are the illustrious acquaintances of Marlow's aunt but important people in the administration of the company?

Thus he regards Marlow with the same grudging, rueful admiration as he does Kurtz. The "new gang of virtue," he calls them, which has a delicious irony because Marlow on his journey to Kurtz is becoming increasingly the imposter of virtue. To the brickmaker, "gang of virtue" suggests merely personal enemy, albeit "of genuinely higher intelligence" and wider sympathy. Marlow, after all, has come upon the scene for the express purpose of relieving or rescuing Kurtz, and thus of sabotaging the plans of the manager and his protégé. His standoffishness and noli-me-tangere superiority to the other agents seems a final, absolute proof that he belongs to a new elite. The brickmaker questions him to find out whether his fears are justified, and Marlow pauses in his narration in an effort to account for the inexplicable bond of sympathy he feels for Kurtz, incredible because the man was no more than a name to him. Nevertheless, he has a dreamlike sense of something between them, a predestined tie—which, he says, is why he let the fellow "think what he pleased about the powers that were behind me" (28).

Marlow is in exuberant spirits after having deceived the brickmaker about the extent of his influence in the company. He thinks it will help him get the rivets he needs to repair his steamboat. He knows in his bones that he is fated to meet Mr. Kurtz, and, on the crest of that emotion, he behaves like a lunatic with the foreman of his mechanics, slapping him on the back and shouting, "We shall have rivets!" (30) and then capering with him in a jig on the iron deck.

But his high-strung mood has accentuated his anxiety about himself, and about his reasons for having stayed on in Africa. Thinking of Kurtz out there in the heart of that jungle, and gazing inwardly at his own dark motives for having come to Africa, Marlow recalls an anecdote about a Scottish sailmaker who fancied that people lived on Mars. When asked how they looked and behaved, the answer came, "walking on all-fours" (27). Since the image of a man crawling on all fours is Kurtz, the implication is that Marlow has become dimly aware of his own bestiality: that his unconscious motive for having come to Africa and having remained is the same as Kurtz's. In his struggle for self-restraint, which is the struggle to suppress the Kurtz within himself, Marlow tries to absolve himself of responsibility for any future actions. The wilderness is at fault—it exerts an actively malevolent influence of "brutal instincts" and "monstrous passions." Concurrently, Marlow begins to see his jungle journey to Kurtz as a passage to primordial man. The invention of these fancies—that the wilderness is a malevolent influence, and that the journey is a regression to savagery—is an instinctive psychological strategy that serves to exonerate Marlow. Africa and the Africans are responsible for whatever is amiss. The ideological significance of this psychology is found in the mythology of infection and the theory of regression that is derived from it: "If the European acts brutally," McClure sums up the theory, "it is not because of any drives instilled or fostered in him by his own community, but because he has been contaminated by the brutal nature of the people he came to save" (1981, 133).

Marlow is struggling in a losing battle. He cannot maintain his self-control, his moral perspective, and at the same time remain in the employ of the company. Survival under those compromising terms necessitates his becoming callous, which is to say that to the colonizer in Africa, survival and moral consciousness are incompatible. When one struggles against this fact as, one may surmise, Fresleven did, one succeeds only in losing touch with reality. Moral degradation is unavoidable even to the most civilized of European colonizers. This is suggested by a painting done by Kurtz more than a year before at the Central Station, when he was on his way to ivory country. One can infer from his depiction of a sinister figure of Justice without scales the degradation of his idealism (25). So long as he remains a company man, Marlow will experience the same, inevitable degradation. In his efforts to segregate himself from the other colonizers he is like a man treading water, trying to keep from getting wet. But these efforts—his turning his back on the agents of the station, his keeping to his salvage day and night—are worse than futile; they are dishonest. Although his unconscious motive for remaining in Africa is his desire to "walk on all fours," he tells himself that he is there to save Kurtz. This rationalization so artfully disguises the unconscious motive that, though his actions violate every value he respects, the alleged mission to save Kurtz keeps him intact. Even the ugly crudity of a gang of marauders called "the Eldorado Exploring Expedition" does not sufficiently disgust him.

Marlow learns more about the extraordinary Kurtz just before the one natural break in the story—the eight-hundred-mile river journey, two months in duration, to the Inner Station, Kurtz's trading post. In a conversation he overhears between the leader of the expedition and the station manager (the leader's nephew), he discovers that the previous year Kurtz had set out for the Central Station with ivory-laden canoes, but had unaccountably turned back three hundred miles downriver, returning with four paddlers in a dugout. The man left in charge of the cargo reported that Kurtz had been seriously ill, and had not completely recovered. Subsequently, Marlow overhears, there had been nine months of rumors from that outpost, and delays from the Central Station preventing relief. This glimpse of Kurtz excites Marlow, who certainly suspects the reasons for Kurtz's unaccountable return. It is no longer ivory, but his own power over the Africans to which the man is addicted. What Marlow admits to himself, however, can only be guessed.

To the Inner Station

Going up that river was like travelling back to the earliest beginnings of the world, when vegetation rioted on the earth and the big trees were kings. An empty stream, a great silence, an impenetrable forest . . . till you thought yourself bewitched and cut off for ever from everything you had known once—somewhere—far away—in another existence perhaps. . . . And this stillness of life did not in the least resemble a peace. It was the stillness of an implacable force brooding over an inscrutable intention. It looked at you with a vengeful aspect. (34)

Marlow has no time to indulge unsettling feelings. He must keep his whole concentration upon incidents at the surface, holding to the channel, avoiding snags, watching for deadwood to fuel the next day's steaming. His work of keeping the steamer afloat was real, if nothing else was, he tells us. The point of the work was the pride of accomplishment—to know he had done his duty, however difficult—the pride of having been faithful to the task. But can one be proud of having maintained upriver trade for the company? Surely no more so than the chief accountant of the Coastal Station can be proud of having kept his books in apple-pie order. Like the chief accountant, without what he calls "pride in work"—which consists in great part of blind devotion to the task at hand—Marlow probably would have lost his grip upon himself. But has he shut his eyes altogether to the knowledge that his work furthers an evil cause? Is Marlow different from the chief accountant in any significant sense? Conrad's eye is exclusively on the plight of the colonizer.

Four types of moral degeneration are depicted in the novel. The first, that of the pilgrims in general, is characterized by loss of self-restraint, capricious cruelty, obsessive greed, and a general state of languid imbecility. A second type, represented by the chief accountant, differs from the first only in its ability to keep up appearances. The chief accountant is no less morally empty than the manager of the Central Station: the same "little loose dirt" within, but smart-looking, like "a hairdresser's dummy," without (26, 18). A third type, represented by Marlow's predecessor, Captain Fresleven, is the European whose tenacity to survive has been undermined by moral disgust—perhaps terror of or inability to let go of all restraints. This type consists of men of conscience who, in the social vacuum, become unbalanced resisting the emergence of their Kurtz-like desires. Kurtz, the fourth type, is the European of conscience who becomes grotesquely devoted to the satisfaction of his passions.

Work shelters Marlow temporarily from the breakdown represented by Fresleven, much as it shelters the chief accountant from the moral degeneration afflicting the colonizers of type one. But with men like Marlow, colonizers with "conscience," or as they are referred to in the text, "the new gang . . . of virtue" (26)—pride in work is as impossible to sustain as belief in the imperial mission, and inevitably as belief in their own idealism or disinterested love of adventure. Work cannot long shelter Marlow from moral collapse. On the symbolic level, it is the devilish means by which he panders to his unconscious motives for having come to Africa. What is his blind devotion to work all about if not getting the boat to Kurtz?

Marlow's hypocritical pride in his ability to navigate the intricate channels of the Congo creates tremendous anxiety. The symbolism of the journey to Kurtz as regression to savagery suggests the force of Marlow's disgust with himself. As the journey progresses, the Africans come to embody the state of monstrous freedom toward which he feels himself helplessly regressing. The reaction of the people of a river village to the passing of the steamer—"a burst of yells, a whirl of black limbs, a mass of hands clapping, of feet stamping, of bodies swaying, of eyes rolling, under the droop of heavy and motionless foliage" (36) elicits from him words like "prehistoric," "the night of first ages" (36), and reflects his own "remote kinship with this wild and passionate uproar," his own "response to the terrible frankness of that noise" (37). Africans in their free state, as described by Marlow, epitomize not only the primitive condition of humankind, but also an actively demoralizing influence, which a white man coming to Africa must challenge "with his own true stuff—with his own inborn strength" (37).

It is this attitude toward the Africans that persuades Benita Parry that "what the fiction validates is Marlow's conviction that the choice before a stranger exposed to an alien world lies between a rigorous adherence to ethnic identity, which carries the freight of remaining ignorant of the foreign, or embracing the unknown and compromising racial integrity. His way, a posture that was traditionally enjoined by British imperialism on its servants, is opposed to Kurtz's dangerous intimacy with the other" (1983, 34). The closer Marlow comes to admitting his illegitimate desires—his reaching Kurtz—the more he feels "visceral revulsion" (Parry's words) for the Africans; and what ultimately commands the reader's attention is not the evils of colonial imperialism, but the demonic hero who achieves "heroic stature by acknowledging his sin in desecrating the commandments of his civilisation" to not compromise racial integrity. Kurtz is the moral of the story, and Marlow, like Kurtz, is "privileged to confirm the value of what he [Kurtz] had profaned" (Parry 1983, 31).

Conrad himself was not conscious of the racist implications of his symbolism, and certainly did not knowingly subscribe to the colonial myth that Africans are to blame for what white men do to them. Critics puzzled by a symbolism that contradicts the anti-imperialist theme of the novel—which identifies blacks with a seductive evil irresistible to civilized white men—generally attempt to explain it away. They argue that Conrad should not be confused with his persona, and that the story is a depiction of the process by which Conrad came to see and accept the truth about the colonial experience in Africa—a truth toward which Marlow gropes. Conrad's hero has been regarded as a zealous, well-intentioned conservative who attempts to sanctify Britain's efficient imperialism, while Conrad's aim in writing the story, the argument follows, is to undermine the values Marlow represents. Jonah Raskin, to cite an extreme instance, supposes Marlow to be a vehicle for "freaking-out" the establishment. He has all the "hang-ups" of the company man, and the novel plumbs the moral obtuseness of that mentality (1971, 149–61).

On the other hand, some critics see nothing disconcerting about Marlow's depiction of Africans—nothing irreconcilable with the anti-imperialist theme of the novel. To Hawkins the fiction explores the evil consequences of imperialism—"that it [disrupts] indigenous cultures" (1979, 294). The novel, as he reads it, reflects a "basic respect for African life." It does not idealize tribal culture, but rather denounces the Western intervention that disrupted it. Marlow, he says, is essentially sympathetic to the Africans. Although in the language of his time he calls them "niggers" and "savages," he feels that unlike the imperialists, they "require no excuse for being there." Furthermore, by comparison to the savagery of Kurtz and the demented rapacity of the colonizers, the Africans' "uncomplicated savagery [is] a positive relief" (59). Marlow sees them as "prehistoric," but certainly recognizes their humanity. Drums, he thinks, may have "as profound a meaning as the sound of bells in a Christian country" (20). He does what he can to help them—offers a dying man in the "grove of death" a biscuit, blows his steam whistle to prevent the Africans from being shot by the pilgrims. In this manner, Hawkins establishes the fact that Marlow is compassionate. He then proceeds to discriminate between Africans in the novel who have and have not been extensively detribalized by imperialism. The rascally guard of the chain gang, as well as the fireman and helmsman, are among the former; the crew of wood-cutting cannibals is among the latter. Hawkins tells us, for instance, that these cannibals, who were probably Bangalas, were enlisted on the way upriver, and were, when at Kurtz's station, only eight hundred miles from home. The helmsman, on the other hand, trained by Marlow's predecessor, was from a distant coastal tribe. Hawkins's point is that the cannibals have innate restraint, because they have not been "detribalized," whereas the helmsman lacks restraint because he has been. He concludes that when Marlow is ironic in his attitude toward the Africans, his emphasis, and the thematic emphasis of the novel, "is on the failure and subversiveness of the civilizing mission that presumed Africans had to be redeemed" (1979, 296).

But Hawkins's argument does not take into account the following facts. At the Coastal Station, Marlow is appalled by the cruelty to Africans. On the journey upriver to Kurtz, he comes close to confessing hatred of them. Feelings are emerging, "creepy thoughts" and ugly emotions, that he is projecting onto his surroundings. His extreme uneasiness is implied in his overreaction to finding a book in a deserted cabin fifty miles from Kurtz's station. The book is a manual of seamanship, which has been worn with use; the discovery of it deeply moves him, as if the little book by Towson contained the sacred writings of a faith in which he, a believer, had been tottering. It has the effect of proving him right in his struggle to preserve a standard of conduct that had seemed increasingly remote and irrelevant. The book helps him feel more stable, more sane, and strengthens his determination to confront moral responsibility. It is, however, short-lived, for simultaneously he feels an overwhelming desire to abdicate moral responsibility and see the trip as no more than an adventure.

Marlow would like nothing more than to be able to simplify things in this way. As external and internal pressures mount, he tries to adopt an attitude that will relieve him of the persecutions of his conscience. It is revealing that shortly after having found the "holy" book, he ducks the question of his moral responsibility by insinuating that the evil extends far beyond his own personal actions: the heart of the human creature itself is evil. "One gets sometimes such a flash of insight" (39). The "flash of insight" is the uselessness of burdening himself with conscience. It also has bearing on his attitude toward his crew of twenty hungry cannibals. As the steamboat nears Kurtz, he finds himself admiring their restraint in not falling on the five white men and eating them. Such admiration is a strategy for ducking responsibility for his own Kurtz-like desires, and it makes for pointed irony at his own expense when seen in light of an imminent discovery—that the great white chief, Kurtz himself, ought, if appearances be true, to have ornamental scars on his cheeks and polished bone through his lower lip.[12]

A mile and a half from the station the boat is attacked. The helmsman is speared, and bleeds to death on Marlow's shoes, while Marlow steers, repulsing the attack with repeated screechings of the steam whistle. The thought that Kurtz must be dead appalls him, as if he had come all that way for nothing. He confesses then to feeling grieved: "my sorrow had a startling extravagance of emotion" (48). A thousand miles downriver at the "grove of death," he had deferred moral judgment, and had used Kurtz to justify his mission. His vain hope had been that Kurtz would have been worthy of respect, in which case Marlow's doubts about the imperial mission would have been reversed and he himself vindicated. The blow he feels in his disappointment is shame at having harbored such dishonest expectations. The narrator is so disturbed by the vivid recollection of his emotion, the guilt beneath the shame, that he turns in exasperation on his *Nellie* audience. "Here you all are, each moored with two good addresses, like a hulk with two anchors, a butcher round one corner, a policeman round another, excellent appetites, and temperature normal—you hear—normal from year's end to year's end" (48); and then he sputters off into a long digressive break in his narrative. The impression he gives is of a man taken by surprise by the depth of his guilty feelings. He cannot bring himself to approach directly the subject of the "gifted" Mr. Kurtz. Between the narration of the ambush and the arrival at the station, the idea conveyed is of a mind reeling, seeking the right posture to take in relation to the summoning of Kurtz. "They say the hair goes on growing sometimes, but this—ah—specimen was impressively bald. The wilderness had patted him on the head . . . it had caressed him, and—lo!—he had withered" (49).

This is a sinister, cartoonlike image, and reflects Marlow's desire to get a grip on himself by trivializing his sense of alarm, and by putting up a wall of disgust between himself and Kurtz. But he cannot get hold of the thread of his story, and conscious of his haltingly guilty approach to the account of his meeting with Kurtz, he again turns in exasperation on his listeners.

> You can't understand. How could you?—with solid pavement under your feet, surrounded by kind neighbours ready to cheer you or to fall on you, stepping delicately between the butcher and the policeman, in the holy terror of scandal and gallows and lunatic asylums—how can you imagine what particular region of the first ages a man's untrammelled feet may take him into by the way of solitude—utter solitude without a policeman—by the way of silence—utter silence, where no warning voice of a kind neighbour can be heard whispering of public opinion? These little things make all the great difference. (50)

At this point in his narrative, the whole tale, the forty thousand words of Marlow's utterance aboard the *Nellie*, appears an effort not precisely to excuse himself, but to account for his guilt—his moral failing—for having been fascinated with Kurtz. The four thousand words of digression interrupting the narrative a mile and a half from Kurtz's station represent a hectic series of defensive postures. In his struggle to account for his fascination with Kurtz, there is, however, a moment of vision. It is inspired by his recollection of Kurtz's vicious, eloquent report to the International Society for the Suppression of Savage Customs, in the postscript of which he strikes rock-bottom truth about the mission of imperialism: "Exterminate all the brutes." Dropping the special case he had previously made for English imperialism—that it was superior to the imperialistic ventures of England's rivals—Marlow sees that the chief, underlying motive of the European colonizer is to be worshiped as a terrible deity. The shock and indictment of that truth bring him back to the thread of his narrative where he describes an act suggestive of the state of his moral exhaustion.

Suffering from fever, beset on all sides by danger, Marlow reacts to a great temptation to be done with the botherings of his conscience by flinging his blood-soaked, guilt-sickening shoes overboard. The shoes have symbolic value because they are connected in his mind with Kurtz's infamous report and with his own humane feelings for the dying helmsman who has bled all over them. Marlow's conscience needs soothing, and as he resumes the account of the last mile of his journey, the reader feels inclined to sympathize with him. The colonial agents aboard his ship are a despicable lot who would heighten anyone's queasy feeling of nightmare. His helmsman, the one person with whom he has had any human contact—a kind of "partnership," he calls it—has bled to death all over his shoes. Kurtz might be dead. The tribesmen of the area are hostile. His own crew of wood-cutting cannibals is not altogether trustworthy. The steamboat is at its last gasp, and he has a touch of the fever. Furthermore, he is in the interior of a vast wilderness, at the furthest navigable point of the trade, eight hundred miles upriver from headquarters, and two hundred more by caravan from the Coastal Station.

At Kurtz's trading post, the boat is hailed by a young Russian who is a phantom image of the man Marlow himself was before his Congo experience. The Russian ran away from an imposing authority figure to take to the sea, served time in English ships, wandered hither and yon, and of all places, turned up in the Congo, exploring, trading; but was now reconciled with his surrogate father: "He made a point of that" (54). The point is also made of his having "started for the interior with a light heart, and no more idea of what would happen to him than a baby" (54). There are more than faint resemblances to Conrad in these details, and it seems a fair surmise that Conrad intends them to suggest the character Marlow, who comes to the reader with no history whatsoever. In any case, it is evident that this colorful patchwork of rags represents all that Marlow at the moment fervently longs to be: nonjudgmental, fearless, reckless in his infatuations—restored to the innocence he had known before the nightmare journey. The fact that the wilderness has not "corrupted" the young Russian, though he had been wandering through it alone for two years, is owing to his simplicity. He is as impregnably innocent of disturbing meditations and greed as is a playful animal—the little, peeling pug nose and blue eyes honestly telling the whole story.

Marlow thinks of the Russian as a harlequin—a colorful patchwork of experiences with no unifying moral consciousness—and is charmed by the seductive dream of living thoughtlessly; but the dream is treacherous, and he knows with a sinking feeling that its appeal indicates just how morally exhausted he is. The glamorous boy worships Kurtz, a man who has impaled the heads of "rebels" outside his cabin. These are ornamental shrunken heads meant to adorn Mr. Kurtz's leisure. They are not there to perform any function—such as a warning to strangers. Their faces are turned towards Kurtz's windows. In his exalted state, Kurtz has found it unnecessary to barter for ivory, which he takes by force at the head of a small army of Africans.

Marlow's admiration for the glamorous boy must stand against these facts. Infatuated by Kurtz's eloquence, filled with wonder at his ascendancy over the Africans, the Russian represents Marlow's criminal longing to escape moral responsibility for his own actions.

When Kurtz is brought from his cabin on an improvised stretcher, emaciated, his eyes bulging from their sockets, Marlow witnesses his remarkable ascendancy over crowds of armed Africans. Could he have terrified them all with his small arsenal of thunder and lightning into adoring him?

Marlow implies plainly enough that Kurtz has been corrupted by the Africans. One is made to suppose therefore that what they now worship in him is the transfiguration of their most basic instincts. This fantastic conception of the Africans is revealing of Marlow's hysteria. McClintock, for instance, writes that "in his description of the Africans, there are no signs of orderly village life, no hints of routine, domestic communality. . . . One has to remind oneself how remote it is from what would have been the 'actual facts of the case' in the Congo of the time, even if one takes into account the ravages of Belgian rule. Congo Africans were in no sense 'Prehistoric man.' They were not still belonging 'to the beginnings of time,' with 'no inherited experience to teach them as it were,' and were not 'rudimentary souls' " (1984, 49–50). McClintock's conclusion is that the spectacle we are given of Kurtz among the Africans is evidence of Marlow's extreme ideological trauma.

Ian Watt, by contrast, sees nothing implausible in the depiction of Kurtz's Africans. He writes

> There is nothing inherently improbable in Kurtz's having been accorded sacred, if not actually divine, status. It was commonly accorded African kings and chieftains at the time; and J. G. Frazer had shown in *The Golden Bough*, whose first edition came out in 1890, that in such cases the illness or impending departure of such a leader as Kurtz would be regarded as calamitous for his people: "In the kingdom of Congo," Frazer wrote, "there was a supreme pontiff . . . and if he were to die a natural death, they thought that the world would perish." Conrad's picture of Kurtz's career at the inner station, then, is sketchy, but not inherently implausible. (1979, 232–33)

To McClure, the spectacle of Kurtz among his Africans is a symbolic illustration of what happens to the colonizer in Africa. Because he misses the essential intuition—that the spectacle is symbolic of the state of Marlow's "psychic uproar" (McClintock 1984, 51)—McClure finds himself defending the novel against the racist implications of its symbolism and particularly the racist notion that the Africans are responsible for Kurtz's corruption. His aim is to prove that the novel has a sustained, anti-imperialist vision, that its thesis is unambiguous: "the forces that brutalize the European colonial thrive at the heart of European civilization, which cultivates and encourages them" (1981,

143). First he proposes that "Kurtz's corruption . . . has two sources, one explicitly sensual and identified with the Africans, the other aggressive and acquisitive and identified with civilized society. Two orders of motivation, typical of two cultures, conspire to destroy him. But the civilized order is primary; Africa's contribution represents a 'terrible vengeance' for Kurtz's brutal invasion" (141). McClure's second theory attempts to reconcile the anti-imperialist theme of the novel, and what appears to be its racist implications, with yet another explanation of Kurtz's corruption—"one in which Kurtz's rapacious lust for wealth and power and the Africans' cannibalism are revealed to be manifestations of the same basic motive" (141). Kurtz, the symbol of the colonizer in Africa, is "a cannibal gone mad, one whose appetite, unlike that of the African crew, is beyond restraint and satisfaction both" (142). McClure insists that, for the most part, "the Africans are presented with sympathy and respect," and that one must look at Kurtz's corruption as climactic and consonant with the dominant, anti-imperialist theme of the novel, not as reverting to the savagery of primitive people, "but to a savagery that seems instead to bear the 'subtle' marks of a morally bankrupt civilization" (137, 139).

At the climactic point of his story, however, Conrad hardly treats Africans with respect, as McClure suggests; nor are they treated realistically, as Ian Watt insists; rather, the picture that we get is symptomatic of the condition of Marlow's mind. What Marlow is to end up grappling with in his confrontation with Kurtz is his own desire to satiate himself in primitive emotions and to be adored as a god. It is the emergence of these temptations into consciousness that is responsible for his bizarre distortions and hatred of the wilderness and the Africans. Kurtz is carried by his bearers to the steamboat. His possessions include some tons of ivory, a small arsenal of weapons (two shotguns, a rifle, and a revolver), his writings (of which there is a packet of correspondence), and the infamous report. With the remarkable man and his plunder aboard, the manager, in his eagerness to discredit Kurtz, immediately begins to indoctrinate Marlow: "unsound method," "fossil" ivory, "more harm than good," "my duty to point it out in the proper quarter"—with the result that Marlow finds himself "[turning] mentally to Kurtz for relief" (63). "Ah! but it was something to have at least a choice of nightmares" (63). Shortly thereafter he is shocked to find that Kurtz has slipped out of the cabin. The discovery fills him with terror "as if something altogether monstrous, intolerable to thought and odious to the soul, had been thrust upon me unexpectedly" (65). His main desire is "to deal with this shadow by [him]self alone" (66). Kurtz, he correctly surmises, is crawling on all fours on a grassy path through the jungle to one of his unspeakable rites, and Marlow, feeling "strangely cocksure," even "chuckling to [him]self," intercepts him, "as though it had been a boyish game" (66).

What lies behind Marlow's hysteria and the "terrific suggestiveness" of the experience? The implication is that Kurtz represents something still as yet unstated, unmentionable, connected with the sensations of suffocation, burial, odiousness, and nightmarish dream. What is stated has all been suggested earlier: that in his solitude the wilderness "had beguiled [Kurtz's] unlawful soul beyond the bounds of permitted aspirations" (67); that there was no appeal other than to "his own exalted and incredible degradation" (67); that his intelligence was perfectly clear, but that his soul was mad; that he was struggling blindly with himself, not rationally, but in suffering; that Marlow had "for [his] sins, [he] suppose[s], to go through the ordeal of looking into it [him]self" (68); and that the experience destroyed Marlow's faith in humanity.

Marlow's behavior seems more and more powerfully to suggest a fear of letting go—fear, Moser and Daleski would say, of sexual abandon. They suggest that Kurtz is Marlow's fantasy of abandon; but though this may be a shrewd insight into Conrad's neuroses, Kurtz has for Marlow a much broader significance. He is the personification of the nihilistic urge, of the darkness within the civilized ego, that when uncontrolled expresses itself in an insatiable, atavistic appetite for sensation and power. Kurtz, while perhaps an image of Conrad's fearful ambivalence about sex, is also the appalling revelation of Marlow's unconscious motive for having gone to Africa. Yet, when forced by the manager to take sides, Marlow prefers the nightmare temptation represented by Kurtz to the petty devils who have neither boldness nor conscience. Kurtz had dared to be enormous. He was viciously depraved, but he still had some vestige of conscience, was still struggling to believe himself noble-minded and a great man. Moral life, though paradoxically responsible for the intensification of the death wish, exists only in terms of the struggle against it, and Kurtz, for one flickering moment before his death (which is perhaps why Conrad gave him a name meaning "short" in German),[13] triumphs in his struggle to be a moral being. Kurtz is the terrifying, horrifying, fascinating spectre of what could happen to Marlow himself should his civilized inhibitions buckle. *Heart of Darkness* is a journey through and beyond inhibition to a rueful affirmation of its necessity.

Kurtz has his moment of truth—of self-revelation and moral judgment, a rending of the veil—just before he dies in the shutter-drawn cabin of the riverboat, and Marlow, who subsequently becomes ill, to "within a hair's-breadth of the last opportunity for pronouncement" (72), declares it a remarkable achievement that having torn through all inhibition, he should have expressed moral judgment with a dying voice. Kurtz's whispered summing-up—"the horror!" (72)—is an affirmation of the need for social restraints, which Marlow finds all the more compelling because of its source. It is not only a call for self-renunciation, duty, and backbreaking devotion to a standard of conduct, but also for the necessity of policemen; and because Marlow has learned from Kurtz to see the necessity of these things as "an affirmation, a moral victory" (72), he feels a debt of obligation to him.

The Return.   The dubious "victory," however, is made to appear tragically sad, a dark necessity, as we observe Marlow, no longer young and ebullient after his return to Europe, but a man older, cynical and embittered. Just how embittered is suggested by his fierce loyalty to Kurtz; for Marlow is still grieving beside the freshly dug grave of his own buried life, grieving over what he knows must be suppressed. Necessity does not preclude sorrow. But sorrow is not quite right: it is sorrow exasperated by rueful self-knowledge. The vision he has acquired, his enlightenment, is tragic because it implies a metaphysical conception developed in Freud's *Civilization and Its Discontents;* namely, that the social inhibitions that are the bedrock of civilized life have fostered a powerful death wish, an instinctual need to dominate or to be destroyed. The subjugation of Africa and the attendant condition of bad conscience in colonizers like Marlow must be understood as part of the psychic price society pays, and will continue to pay, for the fruits of civilization. Marlow's enlightenment—his acknowledgment of Kurtz as his alter ego—has left him at a crossroads where he must confront moral annihilation. The loyalty that prompts him to destroy the memorable postscript to Kurtz's report is a complex emotion consisting of shame, self-pity, anger, and spite, born of a despairing resignation and emptiness of heart.

Because Marlow can imagine no remedy to the evil he has seen, and since there is nothing else but to bury out of mind irremediable evil, he resolves to protect Kurtz's Intended from the truth. That, he says, "I would have to keep back alone for the salvation of another soul" (75). Even though he thinks of her as entombed in her illusions—positioned in her "whited sepulchre" exactly like the trading company—Marlow does not tell her the truth. The one truth he tells her is that he knew Kurtz "as well as it is possible for one man to know another" (76). Of course, on one level it would seem barbaric to destroy her passionate devotion, and perhaps the attempt would be futile in any case, it being fortified within a forehead Marlow imagines to be a cliff of pure crystal. Kurtz's Intended will experience her triumph of sentiment. With despair in his heart, Marlow bows his head "before the faith that was in her, before that great and saving illusion that shone with an unearthly glow in the darkness" (77). Despair ought indeed to be in his heart, for he is acquiescing by his silence to abject pessimism: the realization that to be morally conscious is enervating. The actual lie he tells her, that Kurtz died with her name on his lips, is, on the symbolic level, a tribute—or concession—to the triumphant darkness, and the whole of the story appears a dark meditation on civilization as humanity's dubious victory over itself.

Conclusion: Subjective Impressionism, Symbolic Functions, Meaning of Darkness

Conrad's invention of Marlow as narrator gave him the dual advantages of first-person intimacy and anonymity. In order to write about himself or, more precisely, to portray a man resisting self-awareness, he developed an art that freed him from the responsibility of precisely knowing his own intentions. Conrad's mode of narration is impressionistic rather than analytic—it is a record of evasions as well as insights. It describes a protagonist in flight from something undeniably real and terrifying, who at last achieves partial understanding of his past experience. Thus Marlow, the functional narrator, enables Conrad to evoke the entirety of subjective life.

In *The Spoils of Poynton* (1896) and *What Maisie Knew* (1897), Henry James perfected the method of telling a story through the sensitive observations of one of the characters; and Conrad learned this technique from James, whom he addressed as *"maître"*. But James wrote with thorough knowledge of his ends and means. His use of the indirect narrator "[induces] the reader to zero in from every point within the story to view its centre more clearly" (Watt 1979, 209). Conrad's art also zeros in on a center, but that center in *Heart of Darkness*—Marlow's behavior in Africa—is part of a larger symbolic design, and resonates with metaphysical and prophetic implications. Conrad's art is more suggestive, inconclusive, and open-ended than James's.

"Unquestionably the major intellectual innovators of the 1890's," the historian H. Stuart Hughes writes, "were profoundly interested in the problem of irrational motivation in human conduct. They were obsessed, almost intoxicated, with a rediscovery of the nonlogical, the uncivilized, the inexplicable" ([1958] 1977, 35). The 1890s was a decade in which "psychological process had replaced external reality as the most pressing topic for investigation" (66), and whether Conrad knew it, or could admit it, like many of his contemporaries he helped establish "the cult of Dostoyevsky and Nietzsche as the literary heralds of the new era" (34). Conrad's experiments in narrative are efforts to convey a psychology in which the deep-seated self follows a logic of its own.

A close reading of *Heart of Darkness* reveals that the center of the story is Marlow in the act of resisting his compelling instinctual attraction to Africa. Kurtz is but a name to him for the lure of it, the fascination of forbidden desires, about which he is perpetually deceiving himself. No matter where the text is taken up—for instance, the passage in which Marlow is being pumped by the brickmaker at the Central Station—the focus is invariably on Marlow's attempting to account to himself for being in Africa, attempts in which he practices all kinds of evasion. By looking closely at this section of the text, one sees how Conrad reveals Marlow's inner psychology. By showing Marlow both lying and moralizing against lying he enables the reader to make the important discovery that Marlow's detestation of lies is fueled by an unconscious association between lying and cannibalism.

As he walks to his wrecked steamer, accompanied by the brickmaker, two simultaneous trains of thought are recorded: his acid contempt for the traders—"if I tried I could poke my forefinger through him, and would find nothing inside but a little loose dirt, maybe" (26)—and contrasting impressions of the "amazing reality" of the jungle—"great, expectant, mute"—in which the station is but the pinhead of a clearing by a backwater. "I wondered whether the stillness on the face of the immensity looking at us two were meant as an appeal or as a menace" (27). These are the first conscious expressions of his apprehension that the jungle is a living presence capable of inflicting a terrible vengeance on interlopers. The source of his anxiety is the unspoken question: what compels him to stay? Marlow's anxiety grows to traumatic proportions because of his dishonesty, or, to put it more strongly, his criminal evasiveness. He tries to look inward, to understand himself, and finds himself imagining what Kurtz is doing eight hundred miles upriver in the interior. His efforts at honest self-reflection result in his recalling the anecdote about the Scotch sailmaker "who was certain, dead sure, there were people in Mars. If you asked him for some idea how they looked and behaved, he would get shy and mutter something about 'walking on all-fours'" (27). Marlow, narrating to the *Nellie* audience, is startled by the unaccountable aptness of the phrase "walking on all-fours." It is as if he had uncovered something personally shameful. It evokes a fleeting vision of his midnight tussle with Kurtz, putting him momentarily in touch with the source of his own anxiety. This jolts him into recalling the lie he told Kurtz's Intended, an act for which he felt shame but in which he suppressed the truth. The same shift from recognition to suppression is reenacted before his audience when he moralizes about his detestation of lies. The way he talks about lying is evidence of Conrad's subtlety in suggesting Marlow's unconscious psychology. It enables the reader to get an inkling of the horrifying temptation Marlow associates with Kurtz: "There is a taint of death, a flavour of mortality in lies—which is exactly what I hate and detest in the world—what I want to forget. It makes me miserable and sick, like biting something rotten would do" (27).

The suggestion of cannibalism in these phrases expresses the psychological reality that in the act of lying on Kurtz's behalf Marlow is Kurtz's accomplice—that at some level of consciousness he participated in Kurtz's cannibalism. This is why he has suppressed the memory of Africa, and why, in telling his story, though responding to an inner compulsion to tell the truth, we see him invariably evading it.

Marlow admits that he deceived the brickmaker by permitting the man to believe he had connections in the company. He did so for Kurtz's sake. Considering that Marlow also lies for Kurtz by destroying the incriminating postscript to his infamous report, it appears that lying to himself about Kurtz, and for Kurtz, is the substance of his account of Africa. As to why he should be concerned with Kurtz, Marlow cannot answer. "Do you see the story? Do you see anything? It seems to me I am trying to tell you a dream . . . impossible to convey the life-sensation of any given epoch of one's existence—that which makes its truth, its meaning—its subtle and penetrating essence" (27, 28).

Marlow is always to be seen shying away from confronting his own motives directly. After several long, musing pauses, he tells of his efforts to encourage the brickmaker to send to the Coastal Station for rivets: "And several times a week a coast caravan came in with trade goods—ghastly glazed calico that made you shudder only to look at it, glass beads value about a penny a quart, confounded spotted cotton handkerchiefs. And no rivets. Three carriers could have brought all that was wanted to set that steamboat afloat" (28).

Invariably, the richness of descriptive detail in Marlow's narrative, as in this inventory of "rubbishy" goods, is intended to increase our faith in his reliability. Now, apparently, the explanation occurs to him that his lying to the brickmaker was a maneuver—to get him to order the necessary quantity of rivets. The real question of why he continues to work for the company at all remains unvoiced. Instead we see him moralizing, despising the traders, exhibiting his high-mindedness, re-calling what seems a gratuitous anecdote; and here, in connection with the rivets—just as one wonders why, if carriers leave for the Coastal Station once or twice weekly, he is not with them, on his return to Europe—he gives us a story about "an old hippo that had the bad habit of getting out on the bank and roaming at night over the station grounds" (29). Though the pilgrims empty all their rifles at it, the animal seems not to notice. Is this meant as an allegory of his own inexplicable behavior, and of his thick-skinned temperament?

By looking in this way at Marlow's narration, one sees that Conrad's art in *Heart of Darkness* is subjective impressionism. Marlow is its center and the line of the narrative is his reluctant but inevitable prog-ress toward Kurtz. What makes the reader look outward from the center—reflect upon the story as a myth, ponder its metaphysical sig-nificance—is Conrad's use of symbolism. Marlow's journey to the in-terior of Africa suggests the archetypal journeys of epic literature. In this context, Marlow is Everyman as the questing hero. The darkness he has come to penetrate is both political and psychological.

The image of grass, recurring in several different contexts, suggests the worn path of the colonizer. It is the path that Marlow discovers on his journey. Grass is first seen growing through the skeleton of Marlow's predecessor. It is seen again growing through paving stones of the city from which Marlow embarks. It is identified with the aban-doned villages on the caravan trail to the Central Station, a region deserted by Africans because of the abuses of Europeans. And, finally, it appears when Marlow grapples with the dying Kurtz crawling "on all fours" through wet grass to a midnight orgy, connecting Kurtz's barbaric appetites and Marlow's struggle against his own atavistic impulses.

Another important symbolic motif is that of the human head. Marlow's cranium is measured by the eccentric company doctor. Kurtz's pate has been so polished by the wilderness that it is bone-smooth like ivory. African heads are impaled on posts in front of Kurtz's cabin. The head motif suggests the appalling degeneracy that awaits Marlow at the end of his quest. Similarly, a dramatic, recurrent reference to the long staves carried by the commercial agents conveys a deep, disquieting truth. Marlow ironically calls these adventurers "pilgrims," the staves being emblems to him of imperialism's mission. But the truth about imperialism is revealed in the image of posts, or long staves, on which the shrunken African heads are impaled. Not only rapacious greed, but a darker motive as well, impels the imperialist agents.

Similarly the frame story adds to the novel's density and turns the reader's attention to its metaphysical significance. It is in the frame story that the moral effect of Marlow's African experience is apparent. We see the man he has become before we hear him describe the experience that made him that man. Conrad's narrator is not the sort to protest the evils of imperialism. His tale does not reproach his *Nellie* audience for complicity in colonial crimes. When all is said and done, Marlow, at the story's end, cannot conceive of a more perfect social order, human nature being what it is. He is sick and bitter, but resigned to the status quo. In this respect, Marlow the narrator and Conrad are probably alike. They share certain essential values with Marlow's companions on the *Nellie:* belief in the saving power of hard work, dedication to duty, pride in England, and determination to maintain British supremacy overseas. The effect of the frame story is to impress a moral upon Marlow's narrative: civilization is precious, and perhaps tenuous; therefore, keep faith with the ideals and institutions that support it.

The most elaborate of Conrad's devices for controlling the several dimensions of his story is his metaphorical use of darkness. The novel is about a hero's journey into darkness, his encounter with a nihilistic vision, and his ultimate tribute to an imperfect and tenuous—but necessary—civilizing order. Darkness characterizes the hero's psychological state at each stage of his journey. It functions as a symbol of Marlow's self-enlightenment and political awareness. To interpret its various meanings is to reveal the scope of Conrad's vision and the design of the novel.

The anonymous narrator who sets the scene for Marlow's story observes that British imperialism is something of which to be proud. All the men aboard the *Nellie* share this view. Marlow, however, watching the sunset on the Thames estuary, begins thinking of his experience on the Congo River. The image presented just before he speaks is of darkness settling upon London. It is an unmistakable allusion to the evils of imperialism per se—and may be intended as an ironic comment on the anonymous narrator's tribute to British imperialism. Yet Marlow begins his story with an attempt to describe what the Roman conquest of Britain probably involved—a description in which darkness stands for the savagery, disease, and solitude that threaten the colonizer. What is most acute for Marlow in the pregnant moment before his first words is the memory of his struggle against moral collapse. Darkness, when he first speaks, symbolizes wilderness and implies the colonizer's valor in *la mission civilisatrice*. This concept of the mission of imperialism comes naturally to him as an Englishman. For even after his experience with the ugliness of imperialism, he still embraces the colonial idea, provided the colonies are British. The Belgian colonial enterprise troubles him from the start—although the fact that it was Belgian and not British makes it a sort of fate outside his personal and political responsibility—and his uneasy conscience is implied by his identification of Brussels, the "whited sepulchre," with Jesus' condemnation of the Pharisees in Matthew 23:27–28. His forebodings are given sinister resonance by the retrospective, ironic consciousness of his having been impelled by evil forces from within himself, and by his efforts to whitewash his own behavior in the Congo.

Setting forth, he associates darkness with European civilization and imperialism. Images of entombment, hypocrisy, and vampirism haunt him en route to colonial Africa, and the first stage of his journey, climaxing at the "grove of death," builds to a powerful indictment of the Europeans and their activities. The image of the miragelike French gunboat shelling a continent expresses his sense of absurdity and disorientation. His awe and fear reach a climax at the Coastal Station, creating the impression that in entering the darkness of the colonial lower Congo he enters an overheated catacomb. As Marlow continues his journey, the narration creates and heightens a growing sense of sinister involvement. In the steamer from the "seat of government" to the Coastal Station, Marlow is told of a European's recent suicide. At the company station he turns his back on the brutal and pointless activity of the colonizers, and, hurrying from the chain gang, stumbles into the "grove of death." In his encounter with the bizarre chief accountant there is a further darkness, a darkness of vision in Conrad's failure to understand the implications of his hero's mental state: that, since Marlow never considers quitting or turning back, he is in fact a colonial racist.

As the journey proceeds from the Coastal Station to Kurtz's outpost, darkness increasingly becomes associated with savagery, cannibalism, and human sacrifice, with Africans as the embodiment of these ideas. Marlow is described as journeying not deeper into the macabre hell Europeans have made of the Congo, but into the darkness at the beginnings of time, the darkness of Africa—a regression that threatens his sanity. In telling his story, he describes himself as immune to corrupting influences—a heroic commander. Does he not navigate eight hundred miles of the river's intricate channels without having had the advantage of an apprenticeship? When attacked, it is not he who panics, nor he who fires wildly into the bush, or so forgets himself as to permit his hungry crew of cannibals to eat his helmsman.

Kurtz represents a shocking revelation that the darkness Marlow has penetrated since leaving the Coastal Station is not African, but European. At this moment of truth, Marlow recognizes a powerful temptation within himself to know the gratifications Kurtz has known. The temptation proves too appalling—to "walk on all fours" and glut himself with brutal emotions—and the revelation and the self-knowledge shatter the decent young Englishman. The horror that Marlow imagines Kurtz seeing in the moments before his death focuses his vision on truths about himself, human nature, imperialism, European civilization, and destructive impulses on a large scale. But Marlow is not one to give in to bestiality. Just how he is to live with his nihilistic vision is implied by the lie he tells Kurtz's Intended—irremediable horrors are best buried—and is depicted in the frame story, where he is at his ease among English friends on the sailing yawl. Their consciences are clear, and to them, he is very definitely "one of us."

VI

Levels of Meaning: Debate and Final Word

Political Significance

*H*eart of Darkness has been read as a powerful assault upon imperialism. It has also been attacked, especially of late, as being offensively racist, most blatantly in its depiction of Africans. As early as 1915 Wilson Follett noted that it contained an implicit moral injunction to the white man: keep racial purity. Follett takes *Heart of Darkness* to be a species of Kipling in its preoccupation with "the physical and moral degeneration of the white man in the continent of black or brown men" ([1915] 1966, 56). He interprets it as the tragedy of

> the too intimate understanding of things across the gulf of race. Kurtz, initiated into monstrous and unnameable rites of savages, loses all his bearings in space and time, and slips back into a twilight of chaos like that before mind dawned on the body's bestiality. Evidently Mr. Conrad's philosophy of race anticipates no millennial community wherein the peoples of the earth shall solve their differences by having none. . . . The stories, in every instance, present race as an insoluble enigma, wrapped often, as in *Youth*, with shining vestures of romance, always most alluring of mysteries for the distant beholder secure in his own heritage, but in the nearer view insidious, corrosive, deathly. (56–57)

Follett reads *Heart of Darkness* as a warning to whites: keep your racial heritage pure, or become like Kurtz. Chinua Achebe, the Nigerian novelist, has gone so far as to declare Conrad a "bloody racist" (1979, 319) and *Heart of Darkness* "an offensive and totally deplorable book" (321). He derides Conrad for a "preposterous and perverse kind of arrogance" which "reduc[es] Africa to the role of props for the breakup of one petty European mind" (319).

Conrad has his defenders, politically sophisticated critics of the 1980s, like Hunt Hawkins and John McClure, who argue that his depiction of Africans is on the whole respectful, that "the forces that brutalize the European colonial thrive at the heart of European civilization, which cultivates and encourages them" (McClure 1981, 143), and that his novel has a sustained, anti-imperialist vision.[14]

Benita Parry's reading of *Heart of Darkness*—as an inextricably knotted ambiguity—may represent the most subtle reading of Conrad's political unconscious. She writes:

> the fiction invites a positive response to Marlow's action which its cumulative discussion has countermanded. . . . The address of the primary narrator to a contemporary British audience began with the appearance of flattering their self-esteem as a nation of intrepid and virtuous empire-builders, and ended by disturbing their conscience and undermining their confidence. Marlow on the other hand makes known at the outset his contempt for imperialism's sententious verbiage, and although his narration abundantly validates his view of colonialism as robbery with violence, his story concludes with an affirmation of loyalty to Europe's illusory pure form [Parry here evokes Hawthorn's interpretation of Marlow's lie to Kurtz's Intended]. . . . The fact of the book's existence does give credence to the argument that *Heart of Darkness* is ultimately a public disavowal of imperialism's authorised lies. But although the central dialogue is conducted by Marlow's two voices speaking in counterpoint, one the sardonic and angry dissident denouncing imperialism's means and goals as symptoms of the West's moral decline, the other the devoted member of this world striving to recover a utopian dimension to its apocalyptic ambitions, the fiction's relationship to its principal intelligence is equivocal, giving and withholding authority to his testimony. . . . These discontinuities have evoked conflicting readings and to proffer an interpretation of *Heart of Darkness* as a militant denunciation and a reluctant affirmation of imperialist civilisation, as a fiction that exposes and colludes in imperialism's mystifications, is to recognise its immanent contradictions. (1983, 38–39)

Fredric Jameson, the most prominent Marxist literary critic in America, would argue that there is no ambiguity about the novel's political significance—that in terms of its vision of imperialism, *Heart of Darkness* is, all in all, as innocuous as a slightly poisoned and superlative lollipop. He includes a long chapter on Conrad's narrative method in *The Political Unconscious,* and while his theoretical discussions focus on *Lord Jim* and the Latin world of *Nostromo,* it is easy to infer their application to *Heart of Darkness.* "Today," Jameson says, "when the Third World, and in particular Latin America [Africa in the context of *Heart of Darkness*] speaks in its own literary and political voice, we are better placed to appreciate everything which is offensive and caricatural about Conrad's representation of the politics and the people of Costaguana [the Congo]" (1981, 269–70). Conrad's fiction ideologically distorts the truth in three ways, Jameson says. "At the most general level, we have the classic 'Anglo' picture of a Latin [African] 'race,' lazy, shiftless, and the like [savage, cannibalistic, and the like], to which political order and economic progress must be 'brought' from the outside. This attitude is more complex than simple racism in that it is invested with considerable fantasy-attraction . . . at the same time that it accredits the good opinion the industrial West has of itself" (270). A second level of ideological distortion, Jameson continues, consists of "Conrad's political reflections and attitudes proper" (270). In *Heart of Darkness* he would be sure to criticize such notions as the goodness of British imperialism (and the questionable nature of the imperialism of other countries) and the idea that Western civilization is built upon a primordial savage innocence like that represented by the Congolese depicted in the novel. A third and the most subtle way in which Conrad's narratives transform political reality Jameson explains through "the theory of *ressentiment.*"[15] This theory first proclaims that modernism is a way "to avoid knowing about history" (266)—that is, a way of defusing historical, social, and deeply political impulses—and, second, describes the narrative strategies by which the real content is disguised. Two such strategies, which Jameson describes in discussing *Lord Jim,* he calls melodramatic and metaphysical, respectively. Their application to *Heart of Darkness* follows.

Rather than a radical assault upon imperialism, the novel's subject appears to be the moral collapse of its hero. Jameson would point out that the narrative account of this collapse consists of a melodramatic "overlay of psychoanalytically charged terms and ideological, public slogans" (245), and he would argue that the reader's attention is held to the very end by this pseudoethical level of interpretation. He would probably contend that Kurtz does not liberate the story from innocuousness—and is not the bringer of shattering enlightenment to Marlow—but rather so effectively contributes to transforming Conrad's original political motive for writing the story that the novel succeeds in promoting the politics of imperialism; and he would illustrate this by interpreting the story as Wilson Follett does. The other strategy that Jameson sees Conrad employing, the metaphysical, projects in *Heart of Darkness* the exculpating metaphysic that the "scramble for Africa" was part of the tragic fee the Westerner pays for the privileges of his civilization, and that individual human existence is absurd in face of universal human depravity and the malignant absurdity of nature. This myth enables the reader, so to say, to rewrite the text in a more inoffensive way: namely, that no one is responsible for imperialism, and one need therefore not feel unreasonably guilty. Thus defused, the text offers no particular danger or resistance to the dominant system. Jameson would characterize the narrative method of *Heart of Darkness* as "an anaesthetizing strategy" (230).

Psychoanalytic Interpretations

The writing of fiction, says Bernard Meyer in his psychoanalytic biography of Conrad, is the writer's "achievement through his creative fiction of a corrective revision of a painful reality" (1967, 8). That reality, for the critic seeking understanding of the wishes and fears that lie behind Conrad's art, is a childhood of exceptionally painful memories. Conrad was four years old when his parents were deported to northern Russia for their forbidden political activities. His father, Apollo Korzeniowski, was a landless aristocrat, his family having lost its estates in the 1830 rebellion against Russia. The rebellion was one of a series of efforts at liberation dating back half a century to the partitioning of Poland by Russia, Prussia, and Austria, and was followed in 1863 by another abortive insurrection, one in which Apollo Korzeniowski figured prominently. He helped organize a clandestine committee in Warsaw that evolved into the National Central Committee, which controlled Polish resistance against Russia and was to direct the insurrection of 1863. Apollo took a house in Warsaw in order to be at the center of activity and made it the clandestine meeting place for adherents of revolution. In 1861 he and his wife were tried by a military tribunal and deported seven months later to Vologda in northern Russia.

The cold of Vologda was terrifying to the Korzeniowski family. Barely a year after they arrived, Ewa contracted tuberculosis. The long, tortuous illness gradually reduced her to a shadow. She was thirty-two when she died in April 1865. The seven-year-old boy was shut up with an ailing and melancholy man who "was simply marking time until death would carry him off too" (Meyer 1967, 26). Everything Apollo cared for had been lost or condemned to hopelessness. He would lapse into moods of mysticism touched with despair, or find solace translating Shakespeare and Hugo into Polish. The young Conrad was subject to migraines and nervous fits. Books were his salvation during these years of exile with his father: Shakespeare, Walter Scott, James Fenimore Cooper, stories of the sea by Captain Marryat, tales of exploration by Mungo Park, and Hugo's *The Toilers of the Sea*. "I don't know what would have become of me if I had not been a reading boy," Conrad recounted (quoted in Karl 1979, 75). The boy's only respite from the morbidly claustrophobic atmosphere of his life with his father was a summer visit in 1865 to his maternal uncle's estate in Nowochwastów and his convalescence there from an illness during the winter of 1866. Father and son were finally given permission to leave Vologda, and they resettled in Cracow, Poland, early in 1868. By then Apollo was dying of tuberculosis. The following year, the eleven-year-old boy led the procession at his father's funeral, to which the entire city came to pay tribute to a national hero.

The young Józef's maternal uncle, Tadeusz Bobrowski, who assumed responsibility for the boy, and who remained a stern and loving surrogate parent until his own death, was a lawyer—a solid and dependable citizen. He represented an ethic of dignified and urbane resignation. Bobrowski regarded himself as a patriot, but one whose advocacy was for peaceful reform. Having become guardian of the orphaned son of his poor sister and her dead hero of a husband, he felt obliged to try to obliterate the Korzeniowski influence on the boy. All the Bobrowskis had opposed Ewa's marriage to the quixotic, impoverished, revolutionist poet. Tadeusz blamed Apollo for Ewa's death. The Bobrowskis looked upon the Korzeniowskis as victims of their own fanaticism, and Uncle Tadeusz sought to inculcate in Conrad the sobering virtues of work, duty, renunciation, and the prudent good sense to accept the world as it was, as well as the self-respect to confront it with dignity. For years Bobrowski wrote constantly to Conrad to this end, with special warnings against prodigality. The clash between the two personalities of Conrad's father and uncle may explain the contradictory impulses in the writer: his love of adventure, his simultaneous cultivation of order and self-discipline, his disillusioned pessimism, and his adherence to traditional values. These are the obvious tensions that pervade the whole of Conrad's creative world.

Conrad became bored with school at Cracow. At fifteen he proposed to leave the security of his uncle's guardianship and go to sea. Going to sea was a way of escaping the pressure of having to choose between a radical ideology that he questioned and a middle-class, money-centered accommodation that felt like betrayal. It was a way to step completely outside all "class terrains and see them all equally, from over a great distance, as so much picturesque landscape" (Jameson 1981, 211). Tadeusz tried to dissuade the young Conrad, but even a tour of Switzerland with a tutor expressly charged to wean the youth of his preposterous notions was unsuccessful. He was champing at the bit. Meyer suggests that his determination to go to sea was prompted by a fantasy: the image of himself, "a hesitant and sickly Polish orphan . . . transformed into an impressive, vigorous, and substantial figure—Captain Korzeniowski" (1967, 30). Reality, on the other hand—remaining in Poland—"would have been tantamount to resigning himself to a climate where everyone and everything he had cherished had crumbled, and where he himself might well be the next to perish" (33). Owing to the books he loved, which "saved him from going mad in the midst of all the misery about him, he had learned of another life, and of another world—a world of men, of action, of adventure, and of vitality, a world where death was unknown and man is immortal" (33).

In October 1874, with his guardian's consent, Conrad left Cracow for Marseilles. Tadeusz made him an allowance of two thousand francs a year, and put him in contact with a shipowner, Delestang, with whom Conrad, as a member of the French merchant service, made his first voyages. Between berths in Marseilles, he enjoyed the bohemian café life and seems, through his acquaintance with the Delestangs, to have been at home in artistic circles. He may also, under the influence of the ultraconservative Delestang, have been involved in a plot to set the Pretender Carl back on the throne of Spain. From March to December 1877, he may have sailed on the *Tremolino*, gunrunning from Marseilles to the Spanish coast for the Carlist cause. In all probability, he was involved in smuggling for his own profit. He was reckless, drifting, spending heavily, and in 1877, after quarreling with Delestang, found himself unemployed. His uncle inundated him with letters admonishing him to be more stable.

In early 1878, Conrad attempted suicide. On receiving news that his nephew had had an accident, Bobrowski hastened to Marseilles. The account that Bobrowski gave to everyone—that Conrad was wounded in a duel—was also what Conrad was later to tell his wife Jessie and his friends. Conrad's first biographer also believed this story. But the subsequent discovery of a letter Bobrowski had written to a friend of Conrad's father clearly identifies Conrad's wound as self-inflicted and describes the circumstances that likely prompted the act. Conrad had apparently been involved in a disastrous enterprise on the coast of Spain, had lost sums of money, and was deeply in debt. After having borrowed eight hundred francs, which he gambled away at Monte Carlo, he returned to Marseilles, invited his creditor to tea, and just before his invited guest arrived, shot himself in the chest. He never again made an attempt on his life, but the psychology of suicide and the drama of the act itself are powerfully portrayed in almost all his major fiction.

The critics of Conrad's work who intuit his psychic history from a study of his personal life, and who take for granted, to quote Frederick Crews, "a continuity between the author's psychic life generally and the symbolic world of his fiction" (1967, 510), have offered several highly original interpretations of *Heart of Darkness* based on their psychoanalytic diagnoses.

Gustav Morf was the first of several Conrad biographers to treat the writer psychoanalytically. He argues that Conrad's works are essentially confessional: that their primary impulse is guilt about leaving Poland, and betraying his father, who sacrificed his life for Polish independence. The guilt that tortured him, Morf says, "could be expressed only in an irrational, symbolic form, as we clothe in dreams our most intimate hopes and fears which we dare not avow to others and sometimes not even to ourselves." Morf shows that Conrad's works are ceaselessly haunted by "a vision, always the same, of some exile, some man without a country, some outcast." To the questions, why this recurrent vision; "[w]hy this extraordinary interest in unhappy, uprooted existences? Why this tendency to lay everything to the account of malignant fate?" Morf answers: the need to soothe by confession an unappeasably guilty conscience (1929, 222, 221).

Thomas Moser's analysis of Conrad is also based on an interpretation of what is taken to be the wishes, fears, and anxieties that lie behind Conrad's art. Moser contends that the fundamental impulse behind the recurrent vision that Morf identified is Conrad's symbolic attempt to get to the source of and to break through sexual inhibition. Moser claims that sexual inhibition is manifested throughout the corpus of Conrad's fiction in images and situations that reveal his fear of women. He says that the power of *Heart of Darkness* derives from Conrad's fear of sexual abandon, but that his anxiety has been successfully transmuted into the needs of art; consequently, the imagery born of the author's need to confront his fear does not dominate the novel. Thus, the jungle means much more than female menace. "The jungle stands for 'truth,' for an 'amazing reality.' Conrad equates it with the African natives who alone are full of vitality; the whites are but hollow men. Yet the jungle also means the 'lurking death,' 'profound darkness,' and 'evil,' which belong to the prehistoric life of man, our heritage. We cannot escape this heritage; going into the jungle seems to Marlow like traveling into one's own past, into the world of one's dreams, into the subconscious" (1957, 80). All these evocative meanings, in other words, are stimulated and strengthened by Conrad's attempt to confront his fear of, and fascination with, sex; and because his anxieties about sex have been controlled by the needs of art, "the vegetation imagery means much more than female menace; it means the truth, the darkness, the evil, the death which lie within us, which we must recognize in order to be truly alive" (80).

Moser claims that in *Heart of Darkness* "for the first time Conrad has been able to use material potentially related to sex in such a way as not to ruin his story" (80), but regards the final scene between Marlow and Kurtz's Intended as a partial failure because Marlow's lie weakens the story: "He has made truth seem too important throughout the novel to persuade the reader now to accept falsehood as salvation" (79). What happens in that final scene, according to Moser, is that the old, invariable fear of women does show itself in yet another depiction "of the 'inconceivable triumph' of woman over man." Moser also suggests, however, that Marlow's lie can be seen to represent a successful transmutation of Conrad's anxiety into the needs of art. The lie could be read, for example, "as an indictment of this woman, safe and ignorant in her complacent, Belgian bourgeois existence; she does not *deserve* to hear the truth" (80, 81). The implication of this reading is that Marlow is spunkier and more manly as a consequence of his Congo experience. The lie can also be read as Marlow's reaffirmation of his fellowship with Kurtz: "To accept Kurtz's pronouncement, 'The horror,' means accepting damnation; Marlow's sin, the lie, serves to confirm this" (81). The implication of this reading of the lie is a Marlow more capable of abandon in the future.

Frederick Crews, in line with the approaches developed by Morf and Moser, and responding particularly to Meyer's more faithfully

Freudian biography of Conrad, has written the most diverting of essays, in which he interprets *Heart of Darkness* as an oedipal fantasy. The starting point and stimulus to Crews's astonishing reading of the novel is Meyer's depiction of what he takes to be Conrad's obsessive theme: " 'almost without exception [Meyer points out] Conrad's heroes are motherless wanderers, postponing through momentary bursts of action their long-awaited return to a mother, whose untimely death has sown the seeds of longing and remorse, and whose voice, whispered from beyond the grave, utters her insistent claim upon her son's return.' The fathers of these heroes, like Conrad's own father, tend to have outlived the mothers for a while and then died or departed, leaving the sons to brood over their intimidating high-mindedness and disastrous fanaticism" (1967, 511–12). Crews argues from this intuition of Conrad's psychic history that in the Conradian world manhood is always in doubt; that "duty and discipline and trial constitute a welcome respite from something more fearsome . . . sexuality"; that love relationships that are not a matching of racial opposites are always latently incestuous, and that consequently "heroines tend to be awesome, androgynous, self-sufficient monoliths who can be fought over but not fertilized"; that Conrad's chief antagonist is "the despairing side of his own mind"; that "the real agon in Conrad is the struggle against inhibition"; and that in *Heart of Darkness* the source of his inhibition is "extraordinarily open" (1967, 512, 513–14, 518). Crews then suggests, referring to "the cacophony of explication" of *Heart of Darkness,* "that the appeal of this story cannot rest on its ideas," claiming

> nearly everyone can respond to the symbolic experience at the
> base of his plot and feel the consonance between overt and latent
> emphasis. . . . If such a plot were recounted to a psychoanalyst as
> a dream—and that is just what Marlow calls it—the interpreta-
> tion would be beyond doubt. The exposed sinner at the heart of
> darkness would be an image of the father, accused of sexual
> "rites" with the mother. The dreamer is preoccupied with the pri-
> mal scene, which he symbolically interrupts. The journey into the
> maternal body is both voyeuristic and incestuous, and the rescue

of the father is more defiant and supplantive than tender and restitutive. The closing episode with the "phantom" woman in a sarcophagal setting would be the dreamer-son's squaring of accounts with his dead mother. He "knows" that parental sexuality is entirely the father's fault, and he has preserved the maternal image untarnished by imagining that the father's partner was not she but a savage woman, a personification of the distant country's "colossal body of the fecund and mysterious life." But given the anxiety generated by his fantasy of usurpation, he prefers to suppress the father's misdeeds. Such a tactic reduces the threat of punishment while reestablishing the "pure" mother-son dyad. Only one complaint against the sainted mother is allowed to reach expression: the son tells her with devious truthfulness that the dying sinner's last word ("horror!") [whore] was "your name." (1967, 518, 520)[16]

Marlow's Nihilistic Vision and
Its Bearing on the Meaning of the Novel

J. Hillis Miller interprets *Heart of Darkness* as the work of a man with "double vision." He cites expressions and sentiments from Conrad's *A Personal Record* that he might have taken from any of Conrad's letters to R. B. Cunninghame Graham, words that he believes convey both the truth that Conrad has come to see and the spiritual state of Marlow at the end of *Heart of Darkness*. Conrad writes, "The ethical view of the universe involves us at last in so many cruel and absurd contradictions, where the last vestiges of faith, hope, charity, and even of reason itself, seem ready to perish, that I have come to suspect that the aim of creation cannot be ethical at all" (quoted in Miller 1965, 18). Miller enlarges upon Conrad's words in order to clarify their precise meaning: "A fixed standard of conduct is not a sovereign power enthroned above man. It is his own creation. A man obeying an ethical code is trying to lift himself by his own bootstraps, and by bootstraps which have only an imaginary existence. On the other hand, the tragedy of man's existence lies in the fact that he is cut off irrevocably from the truth of the universe. As long as he remains human he will remain exiled in a nightmarish realm of illusion" (18).

"Double vision" implies wakefulness from the agreeable somnambulism of ordinary life, Miller continues. With this vision, ethical values are seen to be arbitrary and, at best, "sentimental lies." The most cherished of these, that of progress, of humanizing the world, is seen to be vicious hypocrisy. Civilization is itself a lie in that "all human ideals, even the ideal of fidelity, are lies" (17). Miller says that "the aim of all Conrad's fiction is to destroy in the reader his bondage to illusion, and to give him a glimpse of the truth, however dark and disquieting that truth may be" (18, 19). It is to be gathered, then, that Kurtz's deathbed cry "the horror!" is a dramatic, eye-opening moment for Marlow when he finally sees the human condition for what it is. It is a moment of "affirmation" and "moral victory" only in the sense that Marlow, like Kurtz, has the perspicacity and courage to see the truth. From Marlow's newly acquired inner eye, the veil has been lifted. It is in this sense that he is enlightened, and for this reason that he is described in the frame story seated in the lotus posture.

But how is he to live with this newly acquired eye for the truth about reality? What is the meaning of the experience of the narrative for Marlow, and for the reader? Miller writes, "Action which is taken with awareness that the lie is a lie is the only action which is not a mournful and somber delusion" (34). He says further, "Life is the voluntary commitment of one's energies to the fulfillment of a noble idea"; Marlow "confirms his allegiance to civilization by the lie he tells Kurtz's Intended" (33, 34). But Miller then goes on to say that "it is a mistake to define Conrad's solution to the ethical problem by the phrase the 'true lie.' There is nothing true about any action or judgment except their relation to the darkness, and the darkness makes any positive action impossible" (35). Miller's conclusion is that the Conradian hero is given "double vision" only to invariably fall back into agreeable somnambulism and that the penetration and falling back constitute the movement and denouement of the Conradian adventure.

In other words, what we see in the narrator's story of eye-opening revelations (according to Miller) are the contradictions of a man who sees and yet does not see. Miller shows that in the symbolism of light versus darkness, light most consistently represents "the triumph of an unceasing act of will, a will to keep the darkness out and to keep what is within the charmed circle of civilization clear, distinct, and inventoried" (13). Evidently, despite Marlow's "double vision," civilization is represented as the metamorphosis of chaos, irrationality, and the unknown into light, "into clear forms, named and ordered, given a meaning and use by man" (14). Miller points out that the narrator's tendency to think in terms of arming himself against the darkness reveals his commitment to practical Victorian ethics—to the ideal of work, to the conception of duty as steady fidelity to the work at hand, and to the idea of progress as expressed in Charles Kingsley's spirited words about "Brave Young England": "longing to wing its way out of its island prison, to discover and to traffic, to colonise and to civilise, until no wind can sweep the earth which does not bear the echoes of an English voice" (14).

Miller leaves one at the end of his chapter on *Heart of Darkness* thinking of E. M. Forster's and H. L. Mencken's judgments of Conrad. Forster was the first of Conrad's critics to refer specifically to the idea of "double vision" in an effort to put his finger on what irritated him about Conrad. He says, "So there are constant discrepancies between his nearer and his further vision, and here would seem to be the cause of his central obscurity. If he lived only in his experiences, never lifting his eyes to what lies beyond them: or if, having seen what lies beyond, he would subordinate his experiences to it—then in either case he would be easier to read. But he is in neither case. He is too much of a seer to restrain his spirit" ([1936] 1955, 133).

H. L. Mencken is provoked by the sense of "double vision" in Conrad to coin such epithets about him as "cosmic implacability" and "confession of unintelligibility." How, Mencken implies, can there be validity to any human effort that is made the foreground to such a nihilistic vision as Conrad's? Mencken's answer, in referring to the meaning of Marlow's experience in *Heart of Darkness,* is that it can only be, and is, pointless (1917, 16).

Ian Watt arrives at an altogether different conclusion. He says that Conrad's nihilism—the effect of Marlow's having acquired "double vision"—should in theory undermine his commitment to practical Victorian ethics, but in practice gives to it a profoundly human reality. Watt compares Conrad to Freud in that they shared much the same further and nearer vision: of people's destructive instincts and unconscious hatred of civilization on the one hand, and of how they should direct their moral energies ("what seemed most worth their effort") on the other—to "support the modest countertruths on which civilisation depends" (1979, 167).

To T. S. Eliot the nihilistic vision of *Heart of Darkness*—for him a profound and intolerable vision of truth—struck a vital chord. Perhaps Eliot found in the novel a powerful impression of his own despair, and perhaps he also experienced the intimations of a pronounced psychological need for the idea of God. This would explain his allusion to Kurtz, who discovered the horror of civilized life in himself, in the epigraph of the poem "The Hollow Men." It is the transitional poem in the corpus of Eliot's work after which, like Dante, he climbed out of hell and began his expiatory ascent of purgatory, which he imagined the author of *Heart of Darkness* ought to have been about to undertake.

Final Word

If the central idea in *Heart of Darkness* is that Victorian man has fostered within him a psychopathic alter ego—a craving for guiltless, unrestrained freedom—then the motive for imperialism is this craving romanticized. The image of Western society as a sepulchre symbolizes Conrad's idea. It is a hideous conception on two counts: first, in its suggestion that civilized life has become dreary and deathly; and second, that civilization itself is responsible for having fostered a psychopathic craving for destruction. The climax of the novel is the face-to-face encounter between the upright Victorian and the character representing his fantasy of guiltless, unrestrained freedom. Marlow meets in Kurtz a cannibal gone mad from the gratification of every instinctual whim. Whatever we are to make of the midnight abominations, the "unspeakable rites" so shocking to Marlow—and Conrad's awkward hinting at the thing is probably characteristic of the kind of "stylistic reticence" about cannibalism one encounters in Western literature going back to Homer[17]—it is these desires that represent the fundamental motive of imperialism. Kurtz has become, literally, what the colonizer is metaphorically: a cannibal.

Kurtz represents the extreme form of what begins to happen to a certain breed of European—like Marlow, and Fresleven, and the Roman in a toga—when they enter an arena in which they have absolute power, and anything is permissible. They constitute an elite among colonizers. They belong to the "gang of virtue." They are Europeans with conscience. They hold principles and ideals by which they know themselves. They are the representatives of the civilization Conrad depicts as sepulchral. But once in the social vacuum, they find themselves increasingly powerless in the struggle against the loss of their identity, and terrified by the emergence of a new, repugnant self, which they find secretly fascinating. Kurtz represents the unromanticized image of this new self. He has triumphed over the emasculating restraints and hypocrisy of his civilized conscience as if to say, "This is what civilization has fostered! Then let it come." Similar thoughts, we may intuit, passed through Marlow's mind, subverting his judgment, and conspiring with his inadmissible desires, to keep him working for the Belgian company. But the confrontation with Kurtz disgusts him too profoundly for him to continue to fantasize. In Kurtz he confronts something "unmentionable," connected with the sensations of "suffocation," "burial," "odiousness," and "nightmarish dream." That something is the prescience in himself of cannibalistic urges (for if Kurtz is a cannibal, then Marlow has shared these urges). It is what makes him constrict with horror, lie to the Intended, and try to bury out of mind the memory of Africa.

But if there is no remedy for his own suppressed nightmares and for imperialism, what then motivates Marlow to tell his story? One thing seems plain: Marlow's narrative is not meant as a political statement. It is an account, or effort to understand himself, to explain his reprehensible behavior—to get to the source, one may conjecture, of his bad dreams—and is in essence therapeutic—confessional, and, as it turns out, self-exculpatory. Yet, the novel does make a powerful political statement. Marlow's account of himself turns out to be a subtle psychological study of the European in Africa—the loss of self-possession and characteristic dissimulation in the formation of a colonial racist—and it is this ideological portraiture that, on the political level, gives the novel its authenticity and power. Conrad had no idea that his hero was a racist; but that he conceives Marlow as suffering occasionally from bouts of bad conscience is certain. Possibly he is deliberately ironic in making Marlow the narrator the intimate of company men, but if so, it is a bitter irony that can lead only to the nightmare of "double vision." In fact, it is very likely Marlow's unavoidable perception of the irony of his position—the sight of the settling darkness on London making the city appear like a sepulchre while one of his comrades on the *Nellie* is raising a tribute to imperialism—which disturbs him into speech.

It is not politics, but an inner need that makes him speak. For he had learned in Africa that the truth is too horrible to tell, and that it is absolutely necessary, in face of the darkness, for one to shut one's eyes and stand for something; and yet he proceeds to tell his story. Probably Conrad's awkward hinting at cannibalism indicates something personally repugnant, and Marlow's compulsion to get to Kurtz represents Conrad's effort in symbols, in art, to get to the source of his most profound inhibitions. While the literary value of psychoanalytic speculation is debatable, it can give the reader more analytic subtlety.

In any case, whatever it was that motivated Conrad to write *Heart of Darkness,* the narrative describes Marlow's effort to confront the fears he associates with Africa and Kurtz. The narrative dramatizes a struggle in which Marlow cannot bring himself to acknowledge the deep source of his constricting fear and occasional fits of bad conscience. In all probability he will not repeat such tale telling—in which the destructive release of inner truth does no one any good. He will suppress his memories because there is no remedy for his bad dreams, or for Africa, and he will go on enjoying the trust of his imperialist friends.

Notes

1. Karl lists Conrad's complaints after his return from the Congo, through July 1891: "legs swollen, rheumatism in left arm and neuralgia in right arm, stomach in bad condition, hands swollen, nerves disturbed, palpitations of the heart, attacks of suffocation, malarial attack, dyspepsia" (1979, 307).

2. The following excerpt from Stephen Spender's introduction to Malcolm Lowry's *Under the Volcano* seems especially appropriate as an explanation of Marlow's racism. For the consul, suffering from dipsomania, substitute Marlow, suffering from the temptations that kept him in Africa:

> The Consul, then, is a modern hero—or anti-hero—reflecting an extreme external situation within his own extremity. His neurosis becomes diagnosis, not just of himself but of a phase of history. It *is* artistically justified because neurosis, seen not just as one man's case history, but within the context of a wider light, is the dial of the instrument that records the effects of a particular stage of civilisation upon a civilised individual: for the Consul is essentially a man of cultivation. The most sensitive individual, although not the most normal, may provide the most representative expression of a breakdown which affects other people on levels of which they may be scarcely conscious. Yet seeing the needle on the disc of the recording instrument, they know that what it registers is also in some sense their own case. (Spender 1965, xiii–xiv)

3. Earlier, before slavery had destroyed village life, "main streets were lined on both sides with palm trees. Each hut was adorned in a different style, a clever, delightful mingling of wood-carving and matting. The men carried chiselled weapons in bronze and brass. They were clad in multi-coloured stuffs of silk and fibre. Each object, pipe, spoon, or bowl was a work of art" (Frobenius, quoted in Legum 1961, 27).

4. Leopold actually distributed the moneys he accrued from his Congo territories into three separate channels, though only the last of these three was publicly known before his death. The first part of the revenue paid the annuities of certain royal family members; a second part provided the upkeep for Leopold's "superb glasshouses and tropical collections" at Laeken; the final part of the surplus Leopold channelled into a huge fund used for Belgian public works (Ascherson 1963, 274).

5. The "Upriver Book" contains "data and instructions concerning the best passages, dangerous shallows and snags, wooded places where fuel could be collected, visibility orientation points, etc." (Introduction to *Congo Diary*, 3).

6. All quotations from *Heart of Darkness* are taken from the Norton critical edition (1963; reprint ed. New York: 1971) and are cited by page number alone.

7. *Lord Jim* (Boston: Houghton Mifflin, 1958), 33–34.

8. By "skeletalized version of the *Inferno*," Evans means that Conrad follows Dante, in that he has "superimposed on the complicated structure of his ... Hell ... the threefold machinery of Vestibule, Upper Hell, Nether Hell" (1956, 61). The case he makes is very sketchy. He begins by showing that "the close structural parallel between *The Heart of Darkness* and the *Inferno* is not explicit at the Vestibule stage. . . . But from the landing in Africa and Marlow's descent into Limbo the relationship becomes unmistakable" (59). His proof that Conrad modeled the Coastal Station on Dante's Limbo is the Chief Accountant who, Evans argues, resembles the tenants of Dante's Limbo because, like them, he is doomed, but "does not really suffer" (60). Evans continues, "From the coast up the river to the second station the characters in the story ... belong with the lustful, gluttonous, wrathful" of Upper Hell, while the pilgrims of the Central Station belong to "the abode of the fraudulent ... that domain in the *Inferno* of those whose sins of violence and fraud involve exercise of the will." Finally, "at the center of the underworld, Conrad presents Kurtz" who, Evans contends, "fits Dante's scheme perfectly." Kurtz is Lucifer, and like Dante's Lucifer, is a traitor to kindred, to country, to guest, and to God (60).

My own impatience with such schematic approaches to *Heart of Darkness* is well expressed by Ian Watt, who writes, with Evans particularly in mind, that this kind of symbolic interpretation "alerts our attention too exclusively to a few aspects of the narrative" (1979, 191). While Conrad is intentionally suggestive "when he talks of the knitters 'guarding the door of Darkness,' and of the two youths 'being piloted over' " (191), these allusions "are dropped as soon as made; they are not intended to link up with other allusions into a single cryptographic system which gives the main symbolic meaning of the work as a whole" (192).

9. Crews regards Conrad's nihilism as "an oblique assigning of blame for the inhibition which characterizes Conrad's protagonists." Its effect is to blur responsibility: "to think of oneself as helpless within a metaphysical void is to assign an external cause for one's prevailing depression" (1967, 512, 513).

10. Karl tells us that *Blackwood's Magazine* "was the Establishment itself: safe, a conserver of tradition, highly aware of its own esteem, very solicitous about bringing good literature to its readers, and most careful about its selections" (1979, 393). So it is likely that *Blackwood's Magazine* would not have printed a piece critical of British imperialism, and likely they would have defended Conrad in much the same way that T. S. Eliot defended Kipling in writing: "I cannot find any justification for the charge that he held a doctrine of race superiority. He believed that the British have a greater aptitude for ruling than other people, and that they include a greater number of kindly, incorruptible and unself-seeking men capable of administration; and he knew that scepticism in this matter is less likely to lead to greater magnanimity than it is to lead to a relaxation of the sense of responsibility" (from the introduction to *A Choice of Kipling Verse Made by T. S. Eliot* [New York: Scribner's Sons, 1943], 29–30). Could the desire to publish in *Blackwood's Magazine* have affected Conrad's treatment of imperialism?

11. The agents of trade, from Marlow's sardonic perspective, resemble pilgrims. They carry long sticks or staves to emphasize their authority.

12. "The only outright references to cannibalism in *Heart of Darkness* involve black Africans who, in the story, actually refrain from any cannibal act. The irony of that is that the word 'cannibal' is used of black men who don't do it and not of the white man who evidently does" (Rawson 1985, 112).

13. "Kurtz . . . saw clearly beyond the false illusion of his life only at the end; his tragic judgment of himself was a victory, but short—like his name in German" (Wilcox 1960, 13–14).

14. One must add Cedric Watts to Conrad's defenders. His article " 'A Bloody Racist': About Achebe's View of Conrad" in the *Yearbook of English Studies* 13 (1983): 196–209 is an effort to rebut Chinua Achebe point for point.

15. Jameson adopts the term *ressentiment* from Nietzsche, who used it to characterize the inveterate psychology of the Christianized Westerner, which is one of dissimulation—to not betray oneself to oneself—because beneath the surface of pity and pious resignation is a festering ulcer. Nietzsche

is vicious in this singularity of his perception, ever seeing pious ways as ideal-istic cloaks to pathological vulnerability and impotent lust for revenge. Chris-tians, by which he means Westerners en masse, are incurable self-despisers doggedly innocent in their moralistic hypocrisy. They are given to practicing their good Christian ways for essentially two reasons: one, out of hatred of life, in which guise they appear as reprimands incarnate, as though to say that health, soundness, strength, and pride are negative things; and two, to dull the pain of self-perception, that one is "a sick, sickly, crippled animal that has good reasons for being 'tame' " (Nietzsche 1974, 295). Rectitude induces the agreeable feeling of "good conscience," and thus affects the system like a sedative.

Jameson uses Nietzsche's term to suggest that his own analysis of modern literature is no less ruthlessly penetrating—that is, revealing of the true mo-tives of the work behind narrative strategies of concealment.

16. Since writing "The Power of Darkness," Crews has disavowed psy-choanalytic criticism (see Frederick C. Crews, *Out of My System: Psycho-analysis, Ideology, and Critical Method* [New York: Oxford University Press, 1975]).

17. In works such as his book *Order from Confusion Sprung*, (London: Allen & Unwin, 1985), and an article, "Cannibalism and Fiction, Part II: Love and Eating in Fielding, Mailer, Genet and Wittig" *Genre* 11 (1978):227–313, Claude Rawson discusses the effect of taboo subjects—especially cannibal-ism—on literary style. He is currently writing a book on stylistic reticence.

Bibliography

Primary Sources

The Collected Letters of Joseph Conrad. Edited by Frederick Karl. Vol. 1. Cambridge: Cambridge University Press, 1983.

Congo Diary and Other Uncollected Pieces. Edited by Zdzistaw Najder. New York: Doubleday & Co., 1978.

Heart of Darkness. Norton Critical Edition. 1963. Reprint. New York: W. W. Norton & Co., 1971.

Joseph Conrad's Letters to R. B. Cunninghame Graham. Edited by C. T. Watts. Cambridge: Cambridge University Press, 1969.

Letters from Joseph Conrad 1895–1924. Edited by Edward Garnett. Indianapolis: Bobbs-Merrill Co., 1928.

Lord Jim. Boston: Houghton Mifflin, 1958.

A Personal Record. New York: Doubleday & Co., 1924.

Secondary Sources

The works noted by an asterisk contain critical commentaries on *Heart of Darkness* that are discussed in some detail in this book.

Books

Anstey, Roger. *King Leopold's Legacy.* London: Oxford University Press, 1966.

Ascherson, Neal. *The King Incorporated.* London: Allen & Unwin, 1963. This excellent political biography summarizes Leopold's activities in the Congo.

Baumgart, Winifried. *Imperialism.* New York: Oxford University Press, 1982. This work is highly regarded for being well-balanced.

*Beach, Joseph Warren. *The Twentieth Century Novel.* New York: Century Co., 1932.

Crews, Frederick C. *Out of My System: Psychoanalysis, Ideology, and Critical Method.* New York: Oxford University Press, 1975.

*Daleski, H. M. *Joseph Conrad: The Way of Dispossession.* New York: Holmes & Meier, 1977. Daleski's thesis is that Conrad is invariably struggling in his fiction to learn the lesson that true self-possession is based on a "capacity for abandon."

*Follett, Wilson. *Joseph Conrad: A Short Study.* 1915. Reprint. New York: Russell & Russell, 1966. His interpretation of *Heart of Darkness* makes Conrad appear to be a racist.

*Forster, E. M. *Abinger Harvest.* 1936. Reprint. New York: Meridian Books, 1955. His impatience with Conrad's style finds expression in some memorably cutting phrases.

Freud, Sigmund. *Civilization and Its Discontents.* London: Hogarth Press, 1930.

*Guerard, Albert J. *Conrad the Novelist.* 1958. Reprint. Cambridge: Harvard University Press, 1979. This work is one of the most lucid and esteemed studies of Conrad. He reads *Heart of Darkness* as a symbolic journey into self.

*Haugh, R. F. *Joseph Conrad: Discovery in Design.* Norman: University of Oklahoma Press, 1957. Haugh sees Kurtz as the true hero of the story, enabling Marlow to accept the human condition.

*Hawthorn, Jeremy. *Joseph Conrad: Language and Fictional Self-Consciousness.* Lincoln: University of Nebraska Press, 1979. Hawthorn interprets Marlow as the product of an imperialist society that compels his silence and ultimately coopts him.

*Hay, Eloise Knapp. *The Political Novels of Joseph Conrad.* 1963. Reprint. Chicago: University of Chicago Press, 1981.

*Hewitt, Douglas. *Conrad: A Reassessment.* 1952. Reprint. London: Bowes & Bowes, 1969. Hewitt was perhaps the first of Conrad's critics to see Marlow as the focus of *Heart of Darkness* rather than colonialism and Kurtz.

Hughes, H. Stuart. *Consciousness and Society.* 1958. Reprint. New York: Vintage Books, 1977.

*Jameson, Fredric. *The Political Unconscious.* Ithaca, N.Y.: Cornell University Press, 1981. This is the most discussed work of the prominent Marxist literary critic. It contains a long chapter on Conrad with particular emphasis on *Lord Jim* and *Nostromo.*

Karl, Frederick. *Joseph Conrad: The Three Lives.* New York: Farrar, Straus & Giroux, 1979. This superb biography supersedes all previous biographies in most copiously detailing the life of Conrad.

*Leavis, F. R. *The Great Tradition*. 1948. Reprint. Garden City, N.Y.: Doubleday Anchor Books, 1954.

Legum, Colin. *Congo Disaster*. Baltimore: Penguin Books, 1961. Legum's opening chapters offer a lively account of the events leading to the formation of the Congo Free State and of its history under Leopold II.

*McClure, John A. *Kipling and Conrad: The Colonial Fiction*. Cambridge: Harvard University Press, 1981. McClure interprets Conrad's colonial fiction as embodying a consistently sustained anti-imperialist vision remarkably emancipated for its time. He uses classic accounts of colonial psychology (like Octave Mannoni's *Prospero and Caliban: The Psychology of Colonization* [1956; reprint, New York: Praeger, 1964]) in interpreting Conrad's text.

*Mencken, H. L. *A Book of Prefaces*. New York: Alfred A. Knopf, 1917.

Meyer, Bernard. *Joseph Conrad: A Psychoanalytic Biography*. Princeton, N.J.: Princeton University Press, 1967. This is a faithfully Freudian psychoanalytic biography of Conrad, which is sensitive and illuminating.

*Miller, J. Hillis. *Poets of Reality*. Cambridge: Harvard University Press, 1965. Miller strives to define Conrad's nihilistic vision with particular reference to *Heart of Darkness*.

*Morf, Gustav. *The Polish Heritage of Joseph Conrad*. London: Sampson, Low, Marston & Co., 1929.

*Moser, Thomas. *Joseph Conrad: Achievement and Decline*. Cambridge: Harvard University Press, 1957.

Najder, Zdzistaw. *Joseph Conrad: A Chronicle*. New Brunswick, N.J.: Rutgers University Press, 1983. Najder's biography is scrupulously objective and exhaustive. In his review of the work, Frederick Crews claims that "it is the richest and most persuasive portrait of Conrad we have had or will probably ever have."

Nietzsche, Friedrich. *The Gay Science*. Translated by Walter Kaufmann. New York: Random House, 1974.

———. *The Portable Nietzsche*. Translated by Walter Kaufmann. New York: Viking, 1954.

*Parry, Benita. *Conrad and Imperialism: Ideological Boundaries and Visionary Frontiers*. London: Macmillan & Co., 1983. Parry analyzes *Heart of Darkness* as the work of a man with two minds. The mesh of contradictory material indicates that Conrad was not making a political statement.

*Raskin, Jonah. *The Mythology of Imperialism*. New York: Random House, 1971. Raskin claims that Conrad uses Marlow as a vehicle with which to lure his unsuspecting and obtuse readers into a shocking encounter with the truth about imperialism.

Rawson, Claude. *Order from Confusion Sprung: Studies in Eighteenth-Century Literature from Swift to Cowper.* London: Allen & Unwin, 1985.

Russell, Bertrand. *The Autobiography of Bertrand Russell 1872–1914.* Vol. 1. Boston: Little, Brown & Co., 1967.

Sherry, Norman. *Conrad's Western World.* Cambridge: Cambridge University Press, 1971. In his account of Conrad's experience in the Congo, Sherry describes the places Conrad visited, what he likely saw there, and the people he met; he also speculates at length on the probable sources of *Heart of Darkness.*

———. *Conrad: The Critical Heritage.* London: Routledge & Kegan Paul, 1973.

Shestov, Lev. *In Job's Balances.* 1932. Reprint. Athens: Ohio University Press, 1975.

Spender, Stephen. Introduction to *Under the Volcano,* by Malcolm Lowry. 1965. Reprint. New York: New American Library, 1971.

Tennant, Roger. *Joseph Conrad.* New York: Atheneum, 1981. This is an accessible short biography.

*Trilling, Lionel. *Beyond Culture.* New York: Viking, 1965.

Van Ghent, Dorothy. *The English Novel.* New York: Holt, Rinehart & Winston, 1953. This work contains an excellent essay on the "secret sharer" theme in Conrad's works that is useful in elucidating the importance of Kurtz as Marlow's double.

Watt, Ian. *Conrad in the Nineteenth Century.* Berkeley: University of California Press, 1979. This important cultural history examines influences—biographical, philosophical, scientific, and literary—that shaped Conrad's thought and art. It also contains a long commentary on *Heart of Darkness.*

*Woolf, Virginia. *The Common Reader.* New York: Harcourt, Brace & Co., 1925. Woolf comes close to damning Conrad with extravagant praise.

Articles

Achebe, Chinua. "An Image of Africa." In *Chant of Saints: A Gathering of Afro-American Literature, Art, and Scholarship,* edited by Michael S. Harper and Robert B. Stepto, 313–25. Urbana: University of Illinois Press, 1979. Achebe reads *Heart of Darkness* as the best-written Western (racist) novel about Africa.

*Crews, Frederick. "The Power of Darkness." *Partisan Review* 34 (Fall 1967):507–25. Crews offers an astonishing interpretation of the novel as an Oedipal fantasy.

*Evans, Robert O. "Conrad's Underworld." *Modern Fiction Studies* 2, no. 2 (May 1956):56–62. This essay attempts to show Conrad's reliance on Dante.

Feder, Lillian. "Marlow's Descent into Hell." *Nineteenth-Century Fiction* 9, no. 4 (March 1955):280–92. Feder draws an analogy between Marlow's voyage to Africa and Aeneas's descent into the underworld in book 6 of the *Aeneid*.

Hawkins, Hunt. "Conrad and Congolese Exploitation." *Conradiana* 13, no. 2 (1981):94–99.

*———. "Conrad's Critique of Imperialism in *Heart of Darkness*." *PMLA* 94, no. 2 (March 1979):286–99.

———. "The Issue of Racism in *Heart of Darkness*." *Conradiana* 14, no. 3 (1982):163–171. In three excellent essays, Hawkins describes the reality of Belgian colonial Africa and makes connections between *Heart of Darkness* and that history.

McClintock, Anne. " 'Unspeakable Secrets': The Ideology of Landscape in Conrad's *Heart of Darkness*." *Journal of the Midwest Modern Language Association* 17, no. 1 (Spring 1984):38–53. The central intuition of this essay is important: that Marlow's image of Africa is symptomatic of his own moral collapse.

*Ruthven, K. K. "The Savage God: Conrad and Lawrence." *Critical Quarterly* 10, nos. 1 and 2 (Spring/Summer 1968): 39–54. Ruthven sees Kurtz as the hero of the story, and interprets the novel as an attack on the values of Western civilization.

Watts, Cedric. " 'A Bloody Racist': About Achebe's View of Conrad." *Yearbook of English Studies* 13 (1983):196–209. Watts defends the author of *Heart of Darkness* against the charge of racism.

Wilcox, Stewart C. "Conrad's 'Complicated Presentations' of Symbolic Imagery in *Heart of Darkness*." *Philological Quarterly* 39, no. 1 (January 1960):1–17. This excellent essay deals with the symbolic content of the novel.

Index

About the Author

Gary Adelman has been teaching English and European literature for twenty years at the University of Illinois in Urbana-Champaign. He is the author of scholarly articles, a novel, and poems.